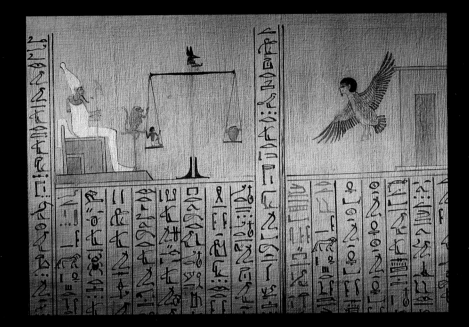

EGYPT

of the Pharaohs

EGYPT
of the Pharaohs

BY BRIAN FAGAN · PHOTOGRAPHS BY KENNETH GARRETT

NATIONAL GEOGRAPHIC

Washington, D.C.

CONTENTS

If you could spend an entire day beside the Great Pyramids of Giza, you would see the sun rise over the Eastern Desert and its light slowly fall on the the face of the Sphinx; then later in the day your own face would shine as you watched the fiery glow of the sun setting in the west behind the pyramids. That single day would convince you that the magic and mystery of ancient Egypt are still very much alive.

I experienced this magic nearly every day for five years when, as a young inspector for the Department of Antiquities, I lived on the Giza plateau with the extraordinary monuments just outside my doorstep. At the spring and autumn equinoxes, I witnessed how the rays of the sun slipped behind the right shoulder of the Sphinx, touching the sanctuary of the Temple of the Sphinx. These magic-filled five years convinced me to dedicate my life to archaeology and to the protection of these eternal monuments.

The same magic took hold of me when I became inspector of antiquities at Abu Simbel. There, twice a year—in October and February—I saw the sun's rays penetrating the depths of the rock-cut temple to light up the faces of statues of two gods and of Ramses II seated at the back of the innermost recess of the temple, while that of another god mysteriously remained in total darkness.

My next assignment was on the west bank at Luxor, where I worked with an expedition from the University of Pennsylvania at the royal palace of the pharaoh Amenhotep III at Malkata, not far from the Valley of the Kings. One morning, something impelled me to visit this place of silence where the kings of the New Kingdom chose to be buried. Alone I entered the tomb of Seti I, the father of Ramses II. The exquisitely colored reliefs from the *Book of the Dead* on its walls made such a deep and mystical impression on me that, even now, I cannot explain it.

When I came back to work at Giza, I began to excavate a water shaft located under the causeway of Khafre's pyramid. This was exactly where, in Roman times, it was believed a tunnel connected the Great Pyramid with the Sphinx. The excavation was difficult, as the shaft was very deep. Our work, at times tedious and exhausting, was shot through with excitement when, at last, we uncovered a large sarcophagus among the remains of four pillars, surrounded by water and interpreted as a cenotaph, or symbolic tomb, of the god Osiris.

A little farther south but still at Giza, in the cliffs at the edge of the desert, we have been excavating the tombs of the pyramid builders. Every day, something ancient comes to light—an inscription, a skeleton, even a potsherd—things that tell the story of the lives of those who

Zahi Hawass at work
in the Valley of the
Golden Mummies,
Bahariya Oasis

labored on the pyramids, things that prove without a doubt that these extraordinary structures were built by the ancient Egyptians, not by slaves, nor even aliens from another world!

In fact, our archaeological work shows that the building of the pyramids must have been a tremendous socializing force in Egypt in these early times: Young conscripts from faraway hamlets and villages were brought to Giza where they were divided into work teams who participated in the construction of the most impressive monuments of the ancient land. The labor of so many people moving so many millions of stone blocks may seem to foreshadow the most dramatic scenes of Cecil B. DeMille's spectacles, yet an even greater drama—the Great Pyramid—still stands majestically on the plateau as a reminder to all the world of their unparalleled cooperative effort.

More recently, news of the surprising discovery of the Valley of the Golden Mummies has fascinated people worldwide. It is the first time an archaeological team has discovered more than 200 mummies, many covered in gold, in only 11 tombs.

Archaeologists from all over the world are working in Egypt, and even with the many recent discoveries—new tombs at Saqqara, the tomb of Ramses II's sons in the Valley of the Kings, the lost cities beneath the sea at Alexandria—we estimate that some 70 percent of the ancient monuments are still buried.

This book, *Egypt of the Pharaohs*, was written by a scholar, Brian Fagan, who has collected all this new information and woven it into a history that is alive and full of adventure. The lavish photographs, made by a friend of mine, Ken Garrett, vividly illustrate the excitement of Egyptian archaeology and the magic of its monuments. I leave you now to live in the lines of history and experience the magic and mystery of ancient Egypt.

Zahi Hawass
Director of the Pyramids
Giza 2001

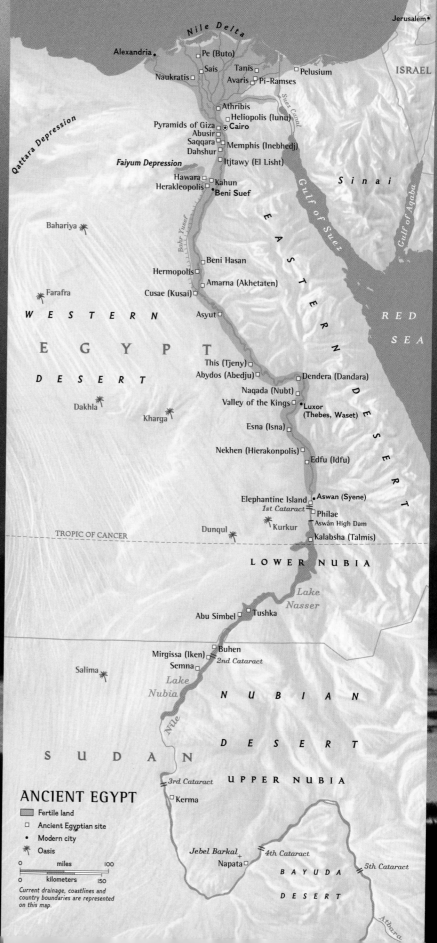

MEDITERRANEAN SEA

Jerusalem•

Nile Delta

ISRAEL

Alexandria•

□ Pe (Buto)
□ Sais   □ Tanis   □ Pelusium
Naukratis □   □ Avaris   Pi-Ramses □

□ Athribis
□ Heliopolis (Iunu)
Pyramids of Giza □ ⊕ Cairo
□ Abusir
Saqqara □ □ Memphis (Inebhedj)
Dahshur □
□ Itjtawy (El Lisht)

Faiyum Depression

Hawara □
Herakleopolis □ □ Kahun
              • Beni Suef

Qattara Depression

S i n a i

Bahariya ✳

□ Beni Hasan
Hermopolis □
□ Amarna (Akhetaten)
Cusae (Kusai) □

Farafra ✳

Asyut □

W E S T E R N

E G Y P T

D E S E R T

Dakhla ✳

Kharga ✳

This (Tjeny) □
Abydos (Abedju) □   □ Dendera (Dandara)
Naqada (Nubt) □
Valley of the Kings □ • Luxor
                    (Thebes, Waset)
Esna (Isna) □
Nekhen (Hierakonpolis) □
                    □ Edfu (Idfu)

Elephantine Island □ • Aswan (Syene)
1st Cataract ⌇   □ Philae
Dunqul •   Kurkur ✳ Aswân High Dam
TROPIC OF CANCER   □ Kalabsha (Talmis)

L O W E R   N U B I A

E A S T E R N   D E S E R T

RED SEA

Gulf of Suez

Suez Canal

Gulf of Aqaba

Lake Nasser

Abu Simbel • □ Tushka

Mirgissa (Iken) □ □ Buhen
Salima ✳   2nd Cataract ⌇
Semna □
Lake Nubia

N U B I A N

D E S E R T

Nile

S U D A N

U P P E R   N U B I A

3rd Cataract ⌇
□ Kerma

ANCIENT EGYPT
▢ Fertile land
□ Ancient Egyptian site
• Modern city
✳ Oasis

0   miles   100
0   kilometers   150

Current drainage, coastlines and country boundaries are represented on this map.

Jebel Barkal + 4th Cataract ⌇
Napata □

B A Y U D A

D E S E R T

5th Cataract ⌇

Atbara

HALF-TITLE PAGE: The god Osiris witnesses the soul of the 18th dynasty royal fan-bearer Maiherpi being weighed on the scales of justice. Maiherpi's funerary papyrus survives as a classic example of the *Book of the Dead,* a guidebook to the afterlife.

TITLE PAGES: Nut, goddess of heaven, stretches across the horizon on the ceiling of King Ramses VI's burial chamber. The dead ruler ascended into the protection of her abode.

OPPOSITE THE TABLE OF CONTENTS: A bearer brings offerings in the tomb of the Old Kingdom sage Ptahhotep (ca 2360 B.C.). Ptahhotep's sayings, much quoted, ring true today: "Be a craftsman in speech that thou mayst be strong, for... speech is mightier than all fighting."

PAGES 8-9: A dramatic sunrise near Luxor marks the return of the sun god to his ancient temples at Thebes. The perpetual journey of the sun god Re epitomized the continuity and eternal truths of ancient Egyptian life. Dead kings joined him on his everlasting journey.

PAGES 10-11: Feluccas, Nile sailing boats, glide quietly with the last of the evening breeze near the now-dammed First Cataract. Ancient Egypt's southern boundary lay at Aswan, just below the cataract. Upstream was Nubia, source of gold, silver, and semiprecious stones.

PAGES 12-13: Annihilators of time, the Pyramids of Giza float above the evening haze on the edge of the Nile Valley. In the pharaohs' time, their smooth sides shone brilliantly. Today, the casing stones are gone, robbed to build Cairo's medieval citadel.

PAGES 14-15: New Kingdom general and later pharaoh Horemheb makes ritual offerings to the god Osiris in his Valley of the Kings sepulchre. Horemheb was Pharaoh Tutankhamun's commander-in-chief, served his successor Aye, then ruled as pharaoh from about 1319 to 1292 B.C.

PAGES 16-17: At the great Sun Court at the Temple of Amun, Luxor, a forest of columns, erected by the "sun-king" Amenhotep III (ca 1355 B.C.), resembles a papyrus thicket, like that which surrounded the primordial mound of creation.

PAGES 18-19: A portrait of Pharaoh Tutankhamun, wearing the royal *nemes* headdress, adorns his third golden coffin. The vulture Nekhbet and cobra Wadjit, protectors of Upper and Lower Egypt, rise from his brow. His beard is fashioned of lapis-colored glass. Lapis lazuli and other semiprecious stones blaze on Tutankhamun's neck collar. Two heavy necklaces of red and yellow gold and blue faience imitate tubular beadwork. The pharaoh holds the symbols of kingship, the crossed crook and flail.

BEGINNINGS

A timeless sunrise over the Nile reflects the unchanging

rhythm of millennia. Rebirth at sunrise, youth, adulthood,

old age, and death at sunset—the journey of the sun god across

the heavens from dawn to dusk was the focus of Egyptian

existence for more than 3,000 years. The Nile, like the sun,

also marked the rhythms of life. It has been said that the Nile,

indeed, created Egypt. With its regular inundations, it brought

life-giving moisture and silty fertility to the soil upon which

was built one of the world's greatest civilizations.

Ka

Ro

Narmer

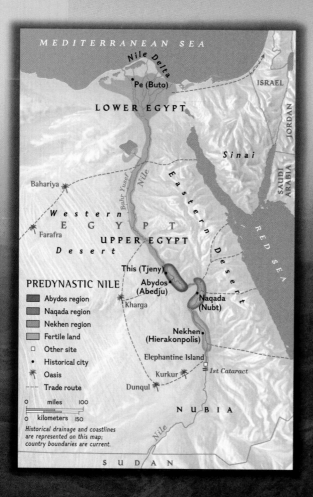

MEDITERRANEAN SEA

Nile Delta

• Pe (Buto)

ISRAEL

LOWER EGYPT

Sinai

JORDAN

Bahariya

Nile

Eastern

SAUDI
ARABIA

Western

E G Y P T

Bahr Yusef

UPPER EGYPT

RED SEA

Farafra

Desert

Desert

This (Tjeny) •

PREDYNASTIC NILE

Abydos
(Abedju) •

Kharga

Naqada
(Nubt)

Abydos region

Naqada region

Nekhen region

Fertile land

Nekhen
(Hierakonpolis)

☐ Other site

• Historical city

✳ Oasis

Elephantine Island

- - - Trade route

Kurkur ✳

☐ 1st Cataract

0   miles   100

Dunqul ✳

0   kilometers   150

N U B I A

Historical drainage and coastlines
are represented on this map;
country boundaries are current.

Nile

S U D A N

BEGINNINGS

The plateau and valleys of the Theban mountains near the
Valley of the Kings west of the Nile are harsh, sterile desert,
the realm of the dead. *Kemet,* the black land, was a long, thin
kingdom hemmed in by the desolate wastes of the eastern
Sahara Desert. Ancient Egypt was like a huge flower. The stalk
formed Upper Egypt; the bloom, the marshy delta of Lower
Egypt. Each summer, the Nile's floodwaters inundated and
fertilized the valley soils. Farmers trapped floodwaters in natural
basins and ponds, then planted their crops. As early as 6000
B.C., perhaps much earlier, dozens of small farming villages
flourished along the river. Within two thousand years, the larger
villages had become small kingdoms, which traded and competed
with one another. After centuries of intense competition,
likened by one expert to a giant game of political Monopoly,
powerful lords from near Abydos in Upper Egypt conquered
their rivals in the delta downstream. They unified Egypt into
a state that endured for nearly three millennia.

A misty dawn on the Nile. The high sails of feluccas flitted like swallows before the gentle north wind. The mist stirred low over the gray water. Palm fronds shimmered gently in the soft breeze. I sat in the bow of our heavily laden craft and watched migrating waterfowl flying high overhead. The voices of men and women walking to their fields broke the morning hush.

A shaft of bright sunlight burst across our sail. The sun god Re had suddenly appeared over the Eastern Desert, washing his land with brilliant rays. I realized that the same rhythms of rising sun and dispersing mist, of village and fields, the long shadows and rosy light of sunset were as old as ancient Egypt itself.

Farmers cultivate the floodplain near Saqqara. Egypt's early farmers, known by their pottery (Naqada II with boats, top), practiced simple agriculture in the parts of Egypt flooded by the Nile.

Occasional rock engravings, like this Nubian ibex from an unknown age, depict the prey of the remote ancestors of the ancient Egyptians. The ancient hunter-gatherers of the Nile are a shadowy presence. We know of them from innumerable stone tools scattered along the river.

As Re rose in the heavens, I watched an endless frieze of unfolding life along the Nile's banks. The sense of timelessness was overwhelming—men riding on donkeys with their legs barely off the ground, a villager raising a shadoof to irrigate his land, women bending over the growing crops in the fields, workers with baskets on their heads cleaning out an irrigation channel exactly as their forebears did 4,000 years ago. I could easily imagine myself back in the time of the pharaohs, when ancient Egyptian civilization endured for more than 3,000 years.

Egypt is an archaeologist's paradise, a palimpsest of pharaohs, priests, and conquering armies. Green fields and growing cities touch the walls of ancient temples. The Nile's dry climate is kind to artifacts and to the dead, preserving even the most delicate fabrics and other treasures of the past. Huge cemeteries and small royal tombs at Naqada and Abydos tell the story of ancient Egypt's humble beginnings more than 5,000 years ago. The Step Pyramid at Saqqara, built around 2650 B.C., is one of the oldest monumental buildings in the world. Amarna preserves the capital of the heretic pharaoh Akhenaten, who rebelled against the power of the priests more than 1,300 years before Christ. The magnificent temples of Thebes proclaim the holiness of the sun god Re and the military exploits of the great warring kings who adorned his temples. These monuments and countless others tell a compelling story of a long vanished civilization.

The Egyptians themselves knew their civilization was of great antiquity. A thousand years after King Djoser built his Step Pyramid, a scribe, Ahmose, son of Iptah, "came to see the Temple of Djoser. He found it as though heaven were within it, Re rising in it." Religious beliefs changed but little, the same festivals were celebrated year after year, and pharaohs ruled according to the precedent of centuries. A famous harper's song, set down at least 4,000 years ago, speaks of those who had gone before:

What of their places? / Their walls have crumbled, / Their places are gone, / As though they had never been!

Today the orderly world of ancient Egypt is long gone. The temples are silent. The gods have disappeared on the tides of history. The sun god Re is no longer of any account in his own shrines. The chants and invocations, the banners, and the dances of adoration have long been stilled. All that remains are crumbling columns and silent inscriptions massaged by the mocking rays of the sun. Ancient Egypt, however, still grips our imaginations. Consider the so-called curse of the pharaohs, pyramid power, and sun worship. Many people fervently believe that Egyptians developed sophisticated computers, had unusual psychic powers, and possessed an

understanding of astronomy and mathematics far superior to ours. These myths and many others linger in the public consciousness.

Likewise, the mystique of Egypt has captivated travelers for centuries. The Greek writer Herodotus traveled up the Nile in the fifth century B.C., when the country was a Persian province. "It has very many remarkable features and has produced more monuments which beggar description than anywhere else in the world," he wrote. Gullible but infinitely curious, Herodotus described mummification and marveled at the Pyramids of Giza, financed, he claimed, by the Pharaoh Khufu's having forced his daughter to work as a prostitute. Herodotus and many other writers proclaimed Egypt the cradle of all civilization. Roman tourists flocked to the Nile and left their graffiti in the Valley of the Kings, burial place of some of Egypt's most powerful pharaohs.

When General Napoleon Bonaparte invaded the Nile Valley in 1798, he took with him a commission of scientists, who had instructions to study Egypt, ancient and modern. Astounded by what they found, they puzzled over enigmatic hieroglyphs, sketched temples while being fired upon, and ran out of lead pencils along the way. When an army officer found the now famous Rosetta Stone, Napoleon's men realized the inscriptions could unlock the secrets of the pharaohs. He ordered plaster copies sent to scholars all over Europe. Some 20 years passed before a young Frenchman, Jean-François Champollion, burst onto a Paris street, crying, "I've got it," before collapsing from fatigue. The modern science of Egyptology was born at that moment.

Now, more than 180 years later, we possess a remarkable yet incomplete ledger of ancient Egypt. The first archaeologists dug sites like potato patches in search of the large and the spectacular, in direct competition with unscrupulous tomb robbers. The end of that era commenced in the late 19th century, when British Egyptologist William Matthew Flinders Petrie introduced somewhat more rigorous methods and insisted on the importance of small objects. Since then, Egyptology has become a highly specialized field of research that combines modern technology, various fields of science, and sophisticated conservation methods with meticulous recording of inscriptions and decipherment of written records. Thanks to high-tech science, we can x-ray pharaohs' mummies, analyze food residues in clay pots, reconstruct temples with computer graphics, and track down the sources of exotic stones and metals. Medical technology has told us more about the health of some ancient Egyptians than they knew themselves. But despite these staggering advances, much of ancient Egypt remains a mystery.

THE BLACK LAND

Egypt is unlike any other country on Earth—isolated from the outside world by deserts, mountains, and the sea and nourished by the longest river on Earth. The Nile rises in the East African highlands and flows more than 4,000 miles northward to the Mediterranean through some of the world's driest terrain. Less than a quarter of the river lies within Egypt itself. The Egyptians called their homeland *Kemet*, the black land, after the dark fertile soils that nurtured their civilization. Kemet slashes across the eastern Sahara like a green arrow, layers upon layers of rich silt lying in a choked-up gorge that was filled when the Mediterranean Sea rose several hundred feet as the last Ice Age began to wane some 14,000 years ago, causing the Nile to back up and overflow its banks.

No one knew where the river with its creative forces came from. The pharaohs believed the source lay in a subterranean stream that flowed in the underworld.

The Nile's life-giving waters were thought to well to the surface between granite rocks close to the First Cataract, from a cavern under Elephantine Island in the middle of the river, more than 600 miles from the Mediterranean Sea.

Thanks to Victorian explorers Richard Burton, John Speke, and others, we know that the Nile rises not at Elephantine but another 3,400 miles upstream in East Africa. Each summer, heavy monsoon rains in the Ethiopian highlands swell the waters of the Blue Nile and Atbara Rivers. Before the construction of the Aswan High Dam in the 1960s, the silt-heavy flood surged northward, reaching its height between July and September. This was the season of inundation, when the river overflowed its banks and spread over the floodplain. The lowest land lies away from the river, so the water flowed far outward to either side. As the current slowed, the river deposited its silt, then slowly receded.

The river waters fertilized and watered the Egyptians' carefully plotted fields. Lush marshlands and meadows provided food for domesticated animals as well as wild beasts. Waterfowl abounded along the Nile banks; fish teemed in its muddy waters. In a good flood year, the river became a vast shallow lake. Villages and towns became islands. As the Nile rose, farmers would build earthen banks to enclose natural basins as reservoirs, then use irrigation works and canals to spread the flood even farther. The people dreaded an exceptionally high inundation, which would sweep everything before it—cattle, houses, entire villages.

Some years the capricious river barely flooded at all, the victim of droughts far upstream. Weak inundations could result in flood stages so low that the river receded almost at once, meaning that thousands would go hungry.

The pharaohs were well aware of the havoc caused by irregular floods. They employed a small army of scribes to read Nilometers with carefully calibrated steps that measured the rise and fall of the flood at Elephantine and at strategic points downstream. Centuries of observations gave them considerable expertise at predicting flood levels, even if there was little they could do when the inundation was a mere trickle, the fields parched.

Kemet might have seemed like a paradise on Earth, and in many respects it was, compared to other parts of the ancient world. But the Egyptians lived at the mercy of natural forces completely beyond their control. Theirs was a world of flowing waters and fecund soil, of order balanced against unpredictable, menacing chaos. Only the sun, moving from sunrise to sunset across a cloudless sky, was unchanging reality. Egyptian notions of the environment, life, religion, kingship, and government stemmed from their dependence on the Nile's waters.

This Predynastic painted pot from the Naqada I culture of Upper Egypt portrays crocodiles floating in the Nile. Early Egyptians valued finely made pottery and traded the work of expert potters from village to village along the river. Crocodiles abounded in the Nile until tourists in the Victorian era greatly reduced the population by shooting them with repeater rifles.

Egypt is a uniquely linear country. From high in space, Kemet looks somewhat like an enormous lotus flower with roots deep in Africa's heart. The stalk and the flower were the Two Lands of the ancient Egyptians. Ta-shema (Upper Egypt), the stalk, begins at the First Cataract, where the valley is only one-and-a-half miles wide. Beyond Elephantine and the First Cataract lay Nubia, Ta-Seti (the land of the Bowmen), where the river vanished into limitless desert and an alien world, a name earned from the Nubians' prowess as archers and warriors. Upper Egypt is about 500 miles long, often bounded by cliffs. The Nile floodplain is as wide as 11 miles at places like Amarna. Near the pharaoh's capital at Memphis, the stalk became the flower as the river meandered through a vast, silt-choked delta to the sea. Ta-mehu (Lower Egypt) encompassed the delta from the Mediterranean Sea (Wadj-ur, or "the Great Green") upstream to Memphis. Moist, low lying, with low hills, swamps, and lakes, the 8,500-square-mile delta became the breadbasket and vineyard of Egypt. In ancient times the mouth of the Nile was a maze of at least five branches, but now there are only two.

The river was a busy highway. Almost all commerce and most royal business passed up and down the Nile, taking advantage of prevailing winds and the current. The pharaoh himself traveled in state through his domains, from the administrative capital at Memphis upstream about 400 miles to Thebes for major religious festivals or on military expeditions. We can imagine the excitement as the royal barge's great sail billowed in the north wind. The weathered steersman stood high at the stern, guiding the vessel through the deepest channels, the king's Nubian bodyguard silently lining the rails. Along the banks villagers and townspeople gathered to stare at the magnificent sight as the pharaoh passed majestically by, veiled from view in a brightly decorated cabin house amidships. Viziers and high officials stared haughtily out from their barges, sailing a respectful distance from their master, the Lord of the Two Lands. The pharaoh's journey upstream was a slow one, even with favorable winds.

But at inundation time the Nile flowed at about four knots, fast enough for a boat to travel downstream from Thebes to Memphis in two weeks. The river was deep and easily navigable, with depths between 25 to 35 feet. As the flood receded, the current slowed dramatically, to no more than about a knot, so the same passage could take as much as two months, with a constant danger of grounding on sandbanks.

The Egyptian state came into being and endured in part because of this natural highway. But Kemet's linear geography came at a price. Distances were large; communication even at the best of times, slow. Egypt was two lands, two regions very

HARVESTING AND MARKETING

Although not cultivated until nearly a thousand years after the building of the Giza Pyramids, dates—traditionally harvested by barefoot men climbing trees with a rope (above)—cause a modern-day buying frenzy in a busy Saqqara market (left). Bearers swirl past with trays of the fruit for sale in Cairo. Ancient Egyptian town and village markets bustled with buyers and sellers of fruit, grains, and vegetables. A constant din of bargaining, of laughter and gossip, filled the air. Markets meant far more than mere buying and selling. Villagers met relatives or bartered for occasional luxuries like simple copper ornaments. Merchants and small-time traders went from market to market with exotic wares. But food was paramount, especially staples—grains, peas, onions, cucumbers, and figs.

different from one another politically and economically. To hold these two lands together required vigorous, decisive leadership, great political sensitivity, and out-standing personal charisma. With strong rule and unity came harmony, balance, and order. He who ruled a united land was the living personification of the falcon-headed god Horus, symbol of kings. He embodied a unified Upper and Lower Egypt.

King Amenhotep III, perhaps the most magnificent of all pharaohs, erected a stela in about 1360 B.C. at the temple of the sun god Re at Karnak that spelled out his job description. "The living Horus: Strong Bull, Arisen in Truth; Two Ladies: Giver of laws, Pacifier of the Two Lands; Gold-Horus: Great of strength, Smiter of Asiat-ics: the King of Upper and Lower Egypt...Beloved of Amen-Re...Who rejoices as he rules the Two Lands like Re forever." The pharaoh was Egypt.

HORUS AND SETH

Water, earth, and sun—these were the basic elements of the ancient Egyptian world. Their existence began with Nun, the primeval waters of nothing-ness. The god Atum, "the completed one," was the Creator, preeminent over the cosmos. He emerged from the watery chaos and caused "the first moment," raising a mound of solid earth above the waters. Then the life-giving force of the sun, Re, rose over the land to cause the rest of creation.

Atum himself emerged on Earth at the site of his temple in Iunet Mehet, "the pillar," usually referred to by its Greek name, Heliopolis, in Lower Egypt (now a sub-urb of Cairo), where the *benben,* a sacred stone shaped like a miniature angular mound, stood in his shrine. The shining gilded capstones of the Pyramids of Giza were also symbolic primordial tumuli. Atum was male, and he created Shu, preserving force of air and light, and Tefnut, the corrosive force of moisture. They in turn gave birth to Geb (earth) and Nut (sky). Their children were the gods Osiris and Seth and their wives Isis and Nephthys. The first nine gods comprised the Ennead, the celebrated nine deities of Heliopolis, dominant in Egyptian religion. But Re was the supreme manifestation of power, depicted most commonly as a falcon, the most compelling bird in the Egyptian sky.

The sun god moved through creation as if traveling in a boat on the Nile. Each day the journey progressed across the heavens, just as life moved forward. At sunset Re descended into the underworld, where he underwent a physical resurrection.

FOLLOWING PAGES: The endless rhythm of village life still unfolds along the

Nile. Children carry produce from the fields along a palm-lined irrigation canal.

In ancient Egypt, always a rural society, even powerful nobles maintained close

links with their home communities in the countryside.

Without fail Re reappeared at sunrise, giving the Egyptians a guarantee that they, too, would rise after death and maintain their rightful place in the order of the universe:

Hail to you, Re, perfect each day, / Who rises at dawn without failing, / Khepri who wearies himself without toil.... / When you cross the sky all faces see you / When you set you are hidden from their sight.

The origin myth of Atum and the "first moment" lay at the heart of Egyptian belief. But how did their civilization really come into being? Can we untangle what actually happened from a complicated skein of myth, official king lists, and painstakingly collected archaeological information?

Egyptian belief and ideology were based on stable and wise government by pious kings, who presided over a harmonious, almost mythically unified, Two Lands. Precedent from the past governed many of their actions, so it followed that such a history was thought of as an orderly sequence of rulers who passed their kingship from one generation to the next. No epic events, no great heroes, no great moral lessons to be learned, just an orderly line of royal ancestors stretched back to a distant moment when time met the cosmos. During the reign of Ramses II (ca 1279-1213 B.C.), an anonymous scribe compiled a list of all the king's predecessors back to Menes, the first recorded ruler of a unified Egypt. According to this Turin Canon, history went back even further to the time when divine spirits ruled the land. Before the spirits, gods reigned as kings for long periods, the scribe god, Thoth, for no less than 7,726 years!

In the first serious attempt to compile pharaonic history, Manetho, an Egyptian priest at Heliopolis about 280 B.C., in his book *Aegyptiaca,* divided Egypt's many rulers into 31 dynasties starting with Menes. (A dynasty was essentially a royal house that endured longer than the rule of a single king, sometimes for centuries.) Today, archaeology provides a more reliable chronicle, but Manetho's dynasty list, the Turin Canon, and the Palermo Stone form the basis for the modern organization of Egyptian history into 31 pharaonic dynasties beginning in about 3000 B.C.

Pharaohs from Menes onward ruled as Horus, a manifestation of the god of heavenly power and the skies. They were known as Horus Menes, Horus Khufu, and so on. The falcon-headed god symbolized good order, his name deriving from the word *hry,* "he who is above/far from." His antagonist was Seth, a snouted creature with forked tail and tall straight ears, the epitome of chaos and disorder. He brought storms and drought, even foreigners, into the harmonious Nile world. The conflict between Horus and Seth symbolized the struggle between the forces of order and anarchy.

The ceremonial Narmer Palette, dating from about 3000 B.C., commemorates victories of King Narmer. This side of the slate palette shows the triumphant king wearing the White Crown of Upper Egypt as he prepares to smite a captive named Wash with a stone-tipped mace. To the right, a falcon, the Horus-king, holds a delta prisoner's head. A high official carries King Narmer's sandals, at left.

Horus and Seth fought constantly over the right to inherit the kingship from Geb's child, Osiris. An archaic document known as the Memphite Theology tells how Geb, the deity of earth and lord of the gods, mediated between Horus and Seth, ending their quarrel. "He made Seth king of Upper Egypt in the land of Upper Egypt, up to the place where he was born....And Geb made Horus king of Lower Egypt in the land of Lower Egypt, up to the place where his father [Osiris] was drowned, which is 'Division of the Two Lands.'"

The Memphite Theology paints unification as an act of harmony, of the triumph of order over chaos. Science tells us that the actual process of joining Upper and Lower Egypt took many centuries.

PREDYNASTIC CHIEFS

Egypt 6000 B.C. Imagine a lush river valley hemmed in by desert, where the irregular rainfall was enough to support rolling plains of arid grassland. Only a few thousand people lived along the river: hunters, plant gatherers, and fisherfolk who may also have cultivated cereal crops. Occasionally, nomadic cattle herders from the surrounding area come visiting to trade or water their beasts. These desert people lived harsh lives, subsisting off blood and milk from their herds. Their leaders were men of long experience and exceptional ritual ability, who called on the supernatural world to predict rain.

By 5000 B.C. the rains were at best sporadic, so the herders moved eastward into the Nile Valley, bringing their cattle culture and religious beliefs with them. For generations, the nomads interacted with more settled communities, perhaps grazing their cattle on water meadows during ever longer dry spells. The Sahara became so arid that most nomads moved into the valley permanently, perhaps bringing with them new religious ideas such as cattle cults, notions of leaders as strong bulls and herdsmen, and perhaps rituals that led to the worship of the fertility goddess Hathor, in the form of a celestial cow. Desert herders and settled farmers merged and intermarried, forging a distinctive Nile farming culture that changed dramatically within a few centuries. Unfortunately, the river has buried or swept away their settlements, but we can imagine tiny villages of reed shelters and mud huts close to natural basins in the floodplain. The women plant emmer wheat and barley in the damp soil. The men hunt deer at the edge of the floodplain with bows and arrows or spear catfish in shallow pools left by the

On the reverse side of the Narmer Palette, shown here, two mythical beasts

intertwine their necks, perhaps symbolizing unification of the kingdom. Above,

Narmer sports the Red Crown of Lower Egypt as he inspects bound and decapitated

enemies. Below, the conquering pharaoh attacks a walled town like a charging bull.

retreating inundation. The crops ripen rapidly in the hot sun. In the heat of late summer, the farmers carefully breach their dikes and release regulated amounts of water onto their fields. Everything depends on careful water management, on the building of canals and dikes, the drainage of swamps, and other tasks that required fast-moving, cooperative labor.

Every villager accepted the discipline of water control, the backbreaking labor directed by a leader who choreographed their efforts. A tradition of authoritarian leadership, of order and conformity, was already ingrained deep in the Egyptian psyche in an environment where rain was virtually nonexistent and everything depended on the life-giving flood and confident leadership. Already, too, the leader may have been thought of as a herdsman, a strongman.

By 3600 B.C., the first glimmerings of Predynastic civilization appear. Clusters of villages coalesced into larger settlements, like that at Naqada, about 15 miles north of Thebes. Originally, the Naqadans had lived in small hamlets spaced about half a mile apart near areas of exceptionally fertile soil. The villagers soon felled trees and removed thick grass, building dikes and digging drainage canals to reclaim more than four times more land. By 3300 B.C. Naqada was a compact walled town of mud-brick houses separated by narrow alleyways.

In the last decade of the 19th century, Egyptologist Flinders Petrie cleared more than 2,000 graves from cemeteries in the desert behind Naqada. Petrie found most Naqada people were humble folk, laid to rest in shallow graves, wrapped in mats or linen shrouds, accompanied by a few strings of beads or clusters of beautifully made red-and-black clay pots. A few graves contained signs of wealth: animal-shaped palettes for grinding cosmetics and superbly fashioned flint knives that could have been made only by master artisans. Naqada's lords lay in another cemetery southwest of the town, their sepulchres lined with brick and furnished with fine pots and other offerings.

Naqada came under the shadow of a more powerful kingdom upstream. Nekhen (the commonly used Greek name, Hierakonpolis, means "city of the falcon") was venerated as the home of the falcon god Horus and an early center of kingship. Nekhen prospered, the population rose steadily, and the demand for clay pots mushroomed, not only as grave goods but also as standardized containers of several sizes, used to brew wheat beer, a nutritious and mildly alcoholic beverage. A brewery found just north of the growing city produced as much as 300 gallons of beer a day, enough for more than 200 people.

NATURAL HIGHWAY

Feluccas crowd the Nile at Elephantine Island at the
First Cataract, the southern frontier of Predynastic
Egypt (right). Glasslike faience figurines (above) of the
1st dynasty found at Elephantine testify to the ancient
importance of this strategic island at the northern
end of the cataract. Here the ram-headed god Khnum
presided over Egypt's life-giving waters, which nourished her crops. Until the roads and railroads of the
19th century, the Nile was Egypt's only highway.
The pharaohs ruled a kingdom stretched out along the
river, which itself provided the means for regular tours
by the king, accompanied by his high officials. The Nile
also moved regiments, grain, and the stone used for
pyramids and temples. Sailing the river demanded
great skill, especially at low water, when laden vessels
could run aground on sandbanks. Ships used prevailing
northerly winds for travel up the river, but few boats
sailed upstream during the summer inundation, when
floodwaters made voyages laborious.

Much of Nekhen's power came from the close associations between the city's rulers and the local falcon god, probably an early form of Horus. In the center of Nekhen rose Egypt's earliest known temple. An image of the god stood atop a pole in an oval court in front of the shrine. At its foot, makeshift platforms displayed sacrificial offerings: cattle and crocodiles, newborn goats, and river fish, some weighing as much as 385 pounds. Four massive wooden posts, at least 20 feet high, supported the facade of the three-room shrine and its walls of brightly colored mats. The posts can have come only from coniferous forests in faraway Lebanon and been floated up the river. The brilliantly colored temple towered over the huddled buildings of the town, a potent symbol of the patron god of its charismatic rulers. Horus was to become the symbol of Egyptian kingship for more than 3,000 years.

Curving rows of the sand-filled burial places of Nekhen's ruling families lie on the banks of a dry gully named Abu Suffian located outside the town. The sepulchres are humble by the standards of later royal burial places, but impressive for their day. Looters ravaged the cemetery in ancient times, leaving behind them an archaeological puzzle—a jumble of finely made black-topped jars, flint arrowheads, and wooden furniture fragments. Egyptologists Barbara Adams and Michael Hoffman undertook a complex salvage operation, using brushes, trowels, and sophisticated recording equipment. They discovered that the cemetery was a symbolic map of Upper and Lower Egypt, with the dry gully serving as the boundary between the two. They also found the earliest known royal sepulcher in Egypt.

Nekhen was the cradle of Egyptian kingship, but the names of its earliest kings are lost to history. We glimpse them only from occasional scenes on decorated artifacts. A magnificent macehead of polished green-and-white porphyry is one of the earliest symbols of leadership from the Nile Valley. Its owner may have been one of the primordial rulers of legendary Egypt. Another mace head shows a ruler in full ceremonial dress, with a ritual bull's tail, a symbol of kingly authority, hanging from the back of his belt. He wears the White Crown of Upper Egypt and wields a mattock, as if he is about to breach the wall of an irrigation canal to release floodwater. A scorpion dangles before his face, presumably a depiction of his name. Bearers of fans and standards participate in the ceremony as an official prepares to receive the first sod from the dike in a basket. The state barge waits to carry the ruler into the flooded basin once it is filled. He wears only the crown of Upper Egypt, so he probably ruled before the climactic event of unification.

FOLLOWING PAGES: A child scurries through a narrow village doorway in the Dakhla Oasis. In this ancient design, houses made of mud brick with thatched roofs joined to form perimeter walls around a central open area. The few low entryways prevented mounted raiders from entering the village.

UNIFICATION

As late as the fifth millennium B.C. much of the delta was still almost desert. Then the Mediterranean rose to modern levels as part of the final adjustment to warmer temperatures after the last Ice Age, causing the Nile to back up and overflow its banks. By 3500 B.C., growing towns flourished beside the watercourses that dissected the plain, each with its own gods and local rulers. Egyptian legends speak of the "Souls of Pe," legendary Predynastic kings who ruled from a town of that name, now known as Buto. The German Archaeological Institute, under Dina Faltings, located the earliest Predynastic settlement at Buto. First occupied in the fourth millennium B.C., it remained an important center for more than five centuries.

Potsherds are among the least glamorous of all archaeological finds, but at Buto they tell a remarkable story. The first inhabitants used highly distinctive, beautifully made pots adorned with white painted bands that bear a close resemblance to wares made in the Negev Desert, far to the east. Their makers used local Nile clay but manufactured the vessels by throwing clay on a turning device, then forming the walls, a method unknown in the delta at the time. Archaeologist Faltings believes the vessels were made by Canaanite potters who settled at Buto to practice their craft.

Upper and Lower Egypt were different lands with diverse cultures, the one influenced by the desert, the other by regular contacts with Asia. Even before unification, the delta was host to a cosmopolitan world. Every year small caravans of donkeys would arrive in the delta towns from the east, carrying saddlebags laden with exotic seashells, semiprecious stones, or lumps of copper ore from the Palestinian mines in the Sinai Desert. Weatherbeaten ships from the countries bordering on the eastern Mediterranean—the Levant—tied up at Buto's wharves, their bilges lined with clay pots filled with olive oil and wine, long cedar logs stacked on deck. Their crews rolled the precious timber into the river, where waiting boats towed the logs laboriously upstream.

Lower Egypt eventually succumbed to more powerful kingdoms to the south. Ornamented palettes from Nekhen, Abydos, and elsewhere depict chieftains at war, vultures and crows attacking the dead. The surviving kingdoms grew larger and larger.

After Nekhen overtook Naqada, the downstream kingdom of This, centered on a community of that name, achieved dominance over Nekhen by conquest or dynastic marriage. The ruler of This became a king, powerful in war, an expert trader, and a living Horus on Earth. He controlled lucrative trade routes with Lower Egypt and developed his own contacts for wine and other luxuries in the Levant.

A sailor of Nubian heritage rests on the foredeck of his felucca near Aswan. Ancient Egypt raided Nubia, the African kingdom above the First Cataract, and took rich resources of humans and material goods. Sailing vessels still ply the Nile, carrying tourists, building stone, and a myriad of staple commodities. Little-changing river levels, thanks to the Aswan Dam, make Nile voyages easier today.

After the king of This and his successors waged war on the delta cities for control of the trade routes, eventually, one of them conquered the Two Lands and became the first pharaoh of a unified Egypt. Who was this first pharaoh? Some names—Ka, Ro, Narmer—have survived through history but little else. The answers are coming from Abydos, a holy place from the earliest days of Egypt. The first two dynasties of pharaohs chose to be buried here, almost midway between the First Cataract and the delta and close to their ancestors at This. The royal cemetery became a magnet for 19th-century archaeologists, who dug with abandon through tombs that had already been pillaged in ancient times. Most people assumed there was nothing left to find.

Günter Dreyer of the German Archaeological Institute thought otherwise. In 1988 he excavated a neglected area east of the royal cemetery, where he made a surprising discovery: a brick-lined royal tomb with 12 rooms designed as a house for the otherworld, complete with windows and doors, built for a king who reigned in about 3250 B.C. The unknown monarch had gone to eternity with lavish possessions and ample food supplies. Also, the unknown ruler's scribes were using a well-developed writing system to inventory crop yields, fully 150 years earlier than hitherto suspected.

Who was the mysterious king, who collected tribute from the delta and traded with the Levant? Günter Dreyer noticed that many of the clay vessels have the name Scorpion painted on them and believes this was the king's name. Dreyer's work confirmed that Abydos was the burial ground of the kings of the 1st dynasty.

In 1898 two British Egyptologists digging at Nekhen had found a magnificent ceremonial slate palette dedicated by King Narmer, who ruled somewhat later than Scorpion. No one knew whether the palette commemorated an actual historical event of unification until recently. Günter Dreyer has recovered a tiny ivory label close to King Narmer's long-since plundered Abydos tomb. The sliver bears a sketch of the king smiting an enemy from the delta, depicted as a human head sprouting papyrus reeds. The labels once marked the dates of oil shipments, the years being identified by major events such as Narmer's victory in the delta. This is obviously the same event as that shown on the famous Narmer Palette, suggesting that this was an actual historical conflict. Who, then, unified Egypt? Almost certainly a series of still unknown rulers from Upper Egypt. They, Scorpion and Narmer, belong to a shadowy dynasty O. Narmer's famous victory may have been the decisive moment of conquest, but it was his successor, King Hor-Aha, or Menes, who became the first ruler of a truly unified Egypt in about 3000 B.C.

The sun sets at the base of Pharaoh Khafre's pyramid on the Giza plateau, dwarfing the humans at its foot. Egyptologist Mark Lehner's discovery—that anyone who stands on the axis of the Sphinx temple at the spring or fall equinox sees the sun setting on the corner of Khafre's pyramid—supports archaeologists' understanding that solar alignments were all-important to kings obsessed with immortality.

Dynasty 1

Menes
Djer
Djet
Den
Anedjib
Semerkhet
Qa'a

Dynasty 2

Hotepsekhemwy
Reneb
Nynetjer
Peribsen
Sekhemib
Khasekhemwy

Dynasty 3

Djoser
Nebka I
Khaba
Huni

Dynasty 4

Snefru
Khufu
Redjedef
Khafre
Nebka II
Menkaure
Shepseskaf

Dynasty 5

Userkaf
Sahure
Neferirkare
Shepseskare
Neferefre
Neuserre
Menkauhor
Djedkare
Unas

Dynasty 6

Teti
Pepi I
Merenre I
Pepi II
Merenre II

Dynasties 7 & 8

Qakare
Neferkaure
Neferkauhor
Neferirkare II

Dynasties 9 & 10

Meryibre
Khety
Merikare
Ity

Dynasty 11

Mentuhotep I
Inyotef I
Inyotef II
Inyotef III

MEDITERRANEAN SEA

Nile Delta

ISRAEL

LOWER EGYPT

Heliopolis
(Iunu)
Giza
Abusir
Saqqara •Memphis (Inebhedj)
Dahshur
Maidum

Sinai

SAUDI ARABIA

JORDAN

Bahariya

Western
E G Y P T
Desert

Farafra

UPPER EGYPT

Eastern Desert

RED SEA

Abydos (Abedju)•

Dakhla

Kharga

Nekhen
(Hierakonpolis)•

Edfu
(Idfu)•

Kurkur

Dunqul

Nile

1st Cataract

OLD KINGDOM

Region of Egyptian control
Fertile land
△ Pyramid site
☐ Other site
• Historical city
✳ Oasis
--- Trade route

*Historical drainage and coastlines
are represented on this map;
country boundaries are current.*

N U B I A

Tushka ☐

| 0 | miles | 100 |
| 0 | kilometers | 150 |

Buhen ☐ 2nd Cataract

Salima

S U D A N

Nubian Desert

THE OLD KINGDOM

Man-made mountains, the Pyramids of Giza brood over modern-day Cairo at sunrise. The pharaohs at their deaths joined the sun god on his journey across the heavens, so their pyramids were viewed as ladders to heaven or as the sun's rays bursting through the clouds and illuminating Earth. For four centuries, the first pharaohs had struggled to hold their kingdom together. Then, in about 2630 B.C., King Djoser's architect Imhotep built the Step Pyramid at Saqqara and began a tradition of royal pyramid building that culminated on the Giza plateau in about 2550 B.C. and endured to the end of the Old Kingdom and beyond. Stone architecture of this scale ushered Egypt into a highly centralized state and had profound effects on its social and political organization. The pharaohs marshaled armies of workers to quarry, hew, and transport stone to build the royal tombs, housing and feeding them during their service. Although these stupendous public works helped create a powerful, prosperous civilization, the effort may have exhausted the kingdom. Later pyramids never rivaled those of Giza. The Old Kingdom ended with the long reign of King Pepi II, whose power, as he grew older, diminished. When drought descended on the Nile Valley in about 2150 B.C., the provincial governors ignored the king and saved their own people from starvation, reigning as virtually independent rulers.

In about 3000 B.C., King Hor-Aha (also called Menes), pharaoh of a unified land, moved his capital downstream to Memphis, the city of the god Ptah, creator god and Lord of Artisans. Ptah's holy city remained the capital of Egypt for many centuries.

Aha was mindful of a powerful local priesthood whose doctrine proclaimed that Ptah's thought, his authoritative utterance, brought the world into being. This seemingly contradicted the widespread belief that Atum, the primordial sun god, was the creator, who emerged from the watery chaos. But Egyptian religion was full of such apparent contradictions.

In Idu's rock-cut tomb in the cemetery east of Khufu's pyramid at Giza, *Ka* statues represent the vital force of the deceased. Idu was supervisor of the mortuary priests who tended Khufu and Khafre's pyramids in Pepi I's time (ca 2260 B.C.). A clasped hand (above) from a standing figure of the official Khufu-Khaf in the same cemetery testifies to the artist's skill.

An Old Kingdom document recording Ptah's deeds—known to Egyptologists as the Memphite Theology—was also inscribed on stone in the eighth century B.C.:

Thus Ptah was satisfied after he had made all things and all divine words. / He gave birth to the gods, / He made the towns, / He established the nomes, / He placed the gods in their shrines.… / Thus were gathered to him all the gods and their kas, / Content, united with the Lord of the Two Lands.

1ST AND 2ND DYNASTIES

Ptah's temple was in Memphis, "The Balance of the Two Worlds," close to the boundary of Upper and Lower Egypt. Unity and kingship resonated from his shrine: "The Great Throne that gives joy to the heart of the gods in the House of Ptah is the granary of Ta-tenen, the mistress of all life, through which the sustenance of the Two Lands is provided.… Osiris came into the earth at the Royal Fortress, to the north of the land to which he had come. His son Horus arose as king of Upper Egypt, arose as king of Lower Egypt, in the embrace of his father Osiris. …"

According to the Greek historian Herodotus, Aha diverted the Nile and built the new city of Memphis behind dikes on politically neutral, reclaimed land. By building the capital on virgin land that symbolized Ptah's mound, Aha became an incarnation of the divine creator at a time when new, more sophisticated religious beliefs came into being. The "White Walls of Menes" surrounding the king's palace gleamed in the Nile sun as a symbol of the divine ruler's power.

The move to Memphis from Nekhen (Hierankonpolis), the ancient southern capital, made good political sense but was an engineer's nightmare. The Nile could make life uncomfortable. In high-flood years, water cascaded over the dikes into the streets. Mud-brick houses melted away as their owners fled to higher ground. Drought years turned the city into desert. Sand blew into the capital and buried dwelling and temple alike. The Nile's channels shifted with the inundations. Here the main river channel moved ever eastward, and the city inevitably moved with the river, its link with the outside world. Aha's capital was soon buried under feet of silt and is now below the water table. David Jeffreys of the Egypt Exploration Society has hand-bored laboriously through layers of silt and discovered a city under siege from changing climatic conditions and irregular Nile floods. The New and Middle Kingdom cities of Memphis occupy two distinct sites, while the archaic capital lies two miles northwest of the surviving city ruins.

According to the priest Manetho, Aha (Menes) reigned over a unified Egypt for 60 years, "made a foreign expedition and won renown, but was killed by a hippopotamus." His successor, Djer, presided over Egypt for 57 years. He campaigned in Nubia as far south as the Second Cataract. An ivory label from a pair of sandals shows another pharaoh, Den, with upraised club smiting an Asiatic captive, an event called "the first time of the smiting of the East." The early pharaohs were men capable of controling a kingdom riven with conflict—a patchwork of competitive provinces.

Menes and his dynastic successors came from Upper Egypt, where desert traditions of leaders as strong bulls and herdsmen ran deep. They were the descendants of tribal shamans or medicine men with supernatural power over the Nile and its life-giving waters. Their ancestors at Nekhen had mediated between the forces of order and chaos, and the new kings followed in the same tradition. Like gods, they kept the forces of evil at bay—the Nubians, Asiatics, and the animals and diseases that preyed on herds and ripening crops. Rulers hunted lions and wild cattle, pursued the hippopotamus, the evil god Seth personified, in the marshes. Human beings were the primary cause of unrest in the Egyptian world. The ideal was *ma'at*, "order" or "right," social justice and moral righteousness, which always existed in opposition to, and in conflict with, *isfet*, the forces of disorder. The Egyptian world was never static, but one of a constant struggle to maintain or enforce order against the forces of chaos, personified by the evil snake god, Apophis, in heaven and Egypt's enemies on Earth.

The rising of the sun each day established order out of the dark chaos of night. For the king ma'at meant keeping order and holding enemies at bay. For people generally, living according to ma'at was living in harmony with others and with the gods. The world was made for the benefit of humans by the creator, who also instituted ma'at at the beginning. An ancient wisdom text advises a later ruler: "Well tended is mankind—god's cattle. He made sky and earth for their sake." Ma'at governed the deeds of every Egyptian pharaoh in an ancient style of leadership that passed from Nekhen to This, from Scorpion to Narmer, and then to Menes and his successors. The kings were the creator incarnate, who returned to him at death.

For decades, the royal cemetery remained at Abydos, where the kings lay in subterranean mud-brick tombs in full regalia with their grave goods, close to a major wadi (dry streambed or gully) leading to the desert mountains. The sepulchre was unmarked except, perhaps, for a low mound and a simple stela. A divine king was immortal, so many of his wives and retainers died with him, to lie in small pit graves around the

Indicative of the wealth of early kings, the falcon face of the god Horus peers fiercely in this 6th dynasty depiction in gold from Nekhen, a cult center for the god (left). In the tomb of the vizier Mereruka at Saqqara (below), busy jewelers labor over a furnace and weigh precious metals with a balance.

tomb of their lord. The practice of human sacrifice survived through the reign of Djer and into the 2nd dynasty before it died out. A separate mud-brick ceremonial enclosure lay above ground, closer to the cultivated land, with a niched facade—called *shunet* in Arabic. The facades were paneled with ornamented recesses that replicated those of the royal palace, as if to create a mansion for eternity. The enclosure served as a form of mortuary temple for the deceased king, including a symbolic primordial mound, a benben, inside.

The sun god, Re, traveled by boat through the sky by day and through the underworld by night, where he was regenerated. So even the earliest pharaohs commissioned funerary craft to carry them symbolically across the heaven with the sun god. In 1988 Egyptologist David O'Connor was exploring a northern sector of the Abydos necropolis when he found lines of mud brick projecting from the desert sand. At first he thought these were buried walls. Excavations three years later revealed an astonishing discovery— 12 boat "graves," each lined and topped with brick, built in a boat shape. Mud plaster and whitewash covered each grave, giving the onlooker an impression of a fleet of white boats floating on symbolic water. A small boulder lay at the bow or stern of several graves, as if representing the anchor. Part of the buried wooden hull of one of the boats had been exposed in 1991, so O'Connor decided to investigate this sepulchre first. In 2000 the excavators probed the center part of the hull and recovered planks and the remains of rope and reed matting. Wood-eating ants had consumed most of the wood, but the outline of the hull was preserved by their telltale frass (excrement). The boat was about 75 feet long and 7 to 10 feet wide at the widest part, with shallow draft and narrow bow and stern, identical in design to the funerary boats buried beside Khufu's Great Pyramid at Giza 400 years later. The Abydos funerary vessels are the earliest known planked boats in the world, their timbers lashed together with rope strung through mortises, the seams caulked with bundles of reeds. These boats are still undated but are estimated to have been built about 3000 B.C., during the 1st dynasty. They all seem to have been buried at the same time, but for which king is still a mystery. Menes or Djer is the most likely candidate. Djer's cult center may lie close by. Whoever their owner, the Abydos boats represent an enormous investment of labor and resources, especially their precious timber planking, to validate divine kings.

For 400 years the earliest pharaohs grappled with the task of consolidating a mosaic of towns and villages scattered along 600 miles of river into a centralized state. The task would challenge even a modern-day government with sophisticated

French Egyptologist Jean-Philippe Lauer, now a nonagenarian, arrived at Saqqara in 1926. For 70 years he has worked to excavate and restore the Step Pyramid site. The complex of courtyards, crypts, temples, and colonnades is a giant illusion made up of dummy buildings. The Egyptians believed that the useless structures with their false doors would come alive in the afterlife and function perfectly.

communications. They succeeded by turning their kingdom into a glorified family business, which flourished on personal loyalty and kin ties and by assuming the mantle of the falcon god Horus. Gods are remote, seldom seen. So were the pharaohs. They dwelt in magnificent palaces surrounded by the trappings of power, their every movement circumscribed by strict protocol. Rare public appearances at festivals were occasions of great importance, symbolizing the rising of the sun at dawn: moments to celebrate a god, give thanks for a victory, or reward high officials.

The pharaoh's official entourage formed the "followers of Horus," loyal officials who surrounded the king in the palace and on his royal tours through the land. They transmitted his commands to the world outside the palace audience chamber. (The word "pharaoh" actually came into use much later, during the New Kingdom, derived from the word *per-aa*, the "great house," after the royal palace).

Over a million people lived in Egypt at unification, a majority in the delta. Most villages and towns lay along the river, separated one from another by cropland and pasture, marshes and thickets. Village headmen brought together the farmers to work on dikes and canals and to dredge natural flood basins. They, in turn, owed allegiance to chieftains, who presided over *nomes*, or tribal provinces, that coincided, in large part, with the natural configurations of the valley. Competition between these nomes had been the crucible for unification. Now the nomes were provinces of a 600-mile-long state, but the ancient network of headmen and chiefly families (nomarchs) still survived. The pharaohs created a system of government that built on these old foundations, placing members of their own family and trusted relatives in positions of high authority, rewarding loyal chieftains by making them governors of their nomes. A small elite governed Egypt for the king, rewarded with titles, emblems of rank, and estates.

The followers of Horus ran the king's household and helped him administer the kingdom. Two high officials were in charge of the Red and White Treasuries, the storehouses of Lower and Upper Egypt. They were ancient equivalents to secretaries of the treasury. Two controllers of the granaries collected and distributed commodities of all kinds, the grain, oil, beer, and other rations paid to everyone who worked for the state, whether official, scribe, or laborer. The overseer of the king's bounty handed out perks to privileged courtiers and officials. From Memphis, the tentacles of administration reached out into towns and villages, through governors, mayors, and headmen, counting, inventorying, taxing, and making decisions. From the beginning, Egypt depended not only on a strong king and competent officials but also on large numbers of scribes.

Scribes formed a part of the literate minority and held a key to power—information. Theirs was an honored profession, writing being an invention of the scribe god Thoth, he of the ibis head. Thus, words had a magical power; the scribe, a special role in the kingdom. Literacy passed from father to son, starting with hesitant glyphs brushed on potsherds and small stones, then on crushed papyrus reed, the paper of ancient Egypt. An essay from later times adjures reluctant pupils: "Be a scribe! your body will be sleek; your hand will be soft.... Set your sight on being a scribe; a fine profession that suits you. You call for one; a thousand answer you."

Ubiquitous scribes were the gear cogs of the kingdom. They were everywhere with pens, palettes, and papyrus rolls: measuring and supervising the harvest, sitting in rows counting baskets of grain loaded into bins, inventorying storerooms. Even the humble seals that once closed granaries and temple stores bear their imprint.

As the state matured, so did the arts of writing and mathematics. The cumbersome glyphs of Menes's time soon developed into a more informal cursive script. Now the scribes could more easily send instructions afar and receive replies, record the heights of Nile floods and send them to Memphis, count the numbers of families and oxen in remote villages. But they needed to make calculations as well—the dimensions

FAMINE AND PLENTY

Children tending family herds in the heavily cultivated fields at Saqqara drive the animals home in the afternoon (left). Today the Aswan High Dam ensures a constant water supply—along with rising salt levels in the soil and serious long-term environmental concerns. Before the dam the Nile was a capricious river and ancient Egyptians lived at the mercy of the inundation. Egyptian priests monitored rising water levels with Nilometers, carefully graded stone steps in the riverbank. Old Kingdom pharaohs were responsible for the regular arrival of the life-giving floodwaters. As living gods their divine powers controlled the river and its waters. During Djoser's reign low floods, and in all probability widespread food shortages, challenged the infallibility of the king. The famine stone from Sehel Island in the First Cataract (above) commemorates a visit by Imhotep during a time of drought. His master, Djoser, had ordered Imhotep to go there and make the normal floodwaters of the Nile return on schedule.

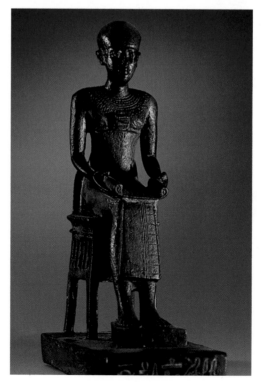

Columns supported by solid walls guard the only true entrance into Djoser's mortuary complex (above). His ka statue (far left) stares out through two small holes in a sealed chamber, perhaps at the northern stars known as the Imperishables. Djoser's architect, Imhotep (left), was worshiped with cult figures for 2,000 years.

of temple floor plans, the size of grain fields, the number of loaves issued to a ship's crew, the quantities of bricks needed for a royal burial chamber. Scribes had to calculate length, width, and volume, compute fractions, survey land, all with a simple linear measure based on the dimensions of the human body and standard units of cubic measurement. The state depended on scribes to monitor the people and their production, and they knew it.

Like all bureaucrats, scribes placed great emphasis on status and titles. Their tombs boast of their achievements with formulaic catalogs of their virtues: "I gave bread to the hungry, clothes [to the naked], I brought the boatless to land," trumpets an official named Sheshi in his Saqqara tomb. In about 2640 B.C., a high official named Hesi-re attached such importance to his tax-collecting duties that he had two elaborate sets of 14 wood-and-leather tubes with strikers for measuring wheat taxes painted on the walls of his tomb. He appears in relief wearing his elaborate wig, carrying his staff of office, with two ink pots slung over his shoulder. A thin elegant mustache adds to his air of authority.

For four centuries the pharaohs wrestled with competing religious agendas. Each nome, each community, had its own deities, despite the divine figure of the king towering over the state. Each ruler juggled loyalties, favored strategic nomes, made diplomatic marriages to cement relationships with potential rivals. They also forged a religious ideology that was to endure for 2,500 years.

From the beginning the 1st and 2nd dynasty pharaohs identified themselves with Horus, "the One on High," a divine force. Their scribes wrote the ruler's name inside a *serekh* panel depicting the facade of his palace with the falcon-headed god perched above, denoting the king as Horus, present, alive, and in residence. Menes also assumed the title, "He of the two Ladies," the cobra of Lower Egypt, the vulture of Upper Egypt.

By 2500 B.C., the king's name appeared within an oval cartouche signifying the circuit of the sun around the universe. The sign, derived from the circular *shen* glyph, also symbolized eternity, thus protecting the king's name, and the king, forever. A second cartouche named the pharaoh Son of Re, identifying his even closer relationship with the sun god.

Supreme rulers thrive on propaganda. So the early pharaohs proclaimed that they maintained order in the presence of a supreme divine force, the power of the sun. The pharaoh's clothing and regalia became a mantle of divinity—of potency in creation. He was herdsman and protector of the people. Each king wore the regalia of a pastoral chief, a *shemset* apron at his waist, his back guarded by a bull's tail hanging

King Snefru's high priest Rahotep and his wife Nofret live on in limestone inside
their mastaba near the Maidum Pyramid. Old Kingdom artists depicted their
subjects with startling realism in the belief that the spirits of the deceased would
recognize their tombs as their homes. The realistic statues terrified the workers
who found them in 1871.

from a belt. He carried the crook and flail of a shepherd, a goat-hair beard on his
chin. By the pharaoh Den's time, the ruler wore a double crown that combined the
red headdress of Lower Egypt and the white of Upper Egypt.

The propaganda of omnipotent kingship rang out in chants and recitations, in elaborate public ceremonies, as hieroglyphic inscriptions on temple and palace walls, in art
and architecture. In art, inscription, and regalia, the king became a warrior and
a builder. He passed the goodness of humankind to heaven and received the blessing of
the creator and the other gods for Earth. The king is seen making offerings to gods, proffering the produce of the land, or, in the case of the 3rd dynasty pharaoh Huni, standing
face-to-face with the falcon-headed Horus. The god clasps the king's forearm with his
left hand, while his right arm encircles the royal shoulders as a sign of protection.

To tour an Egyptian temple is to be bombarded with a constant recitation of divine
kingship: The king in the presence of Osiris, the king making offerings to the sun god Re,
the king offering a figure of the goddess Ma'at, "rightness," to the deities Amun, Re, and
Ptah. The litany soon becomes monotonous but is overwhelming in its repetition. Always the
pharaoh triumphs. He spears a hippopotamus-like Seth in the triumph of good over evil,
holds up the sacred bark of the sun god and hence the cosmos, and slaughters Asiatic foes.

Some years ago I happened to visit the great medieval cathedral of Notre Dame de
Chartres just weeks after spending a day in the sun god Amun's great temple at Karnak
in Thebes. The cathedral is all stained-glass windows, a masterpiece of ethereal forms
set among soaring beams and graceful arches. The windows lay out an image of the Christian cosmos in brilliant color, while a maze on the nave floor depicts the tortuous path
of the human soul through life on Earth. Only about 1,500 people lived in Chartres
when the cathedral was rebuilt after a fire in the late 12th century, but as many as 10,000
flocked to the town on holy days. Like Karnak, Chartres was a site for spectacles and
grand ceremonies, a tangible symbol of eternal, supernatural reality. I remember thinking how its windows, like Karnak's statuary and brightly painted reliefs, instructed the
nonliterate with a standard vocabulary of forms. The message was repeated again and
again on Egypt's public buildings—the pharaoh is divine and infallible; he is eternity.

For all the propaganda, rivalries between north and south bubbled below the surface. In about 2700 B.C. a 2nd dynasty ruler named Sekhemib dropped his Horus name
in favor of a new one: Seth-Peribsen. The age-old conflict between Seth and Horus broke
out again amidst fighting and unrest between north and south. The last pharaoh of the
dynasty, Khasekhem was forced by northern forces to retreat to Nekhen.

The revolt was suppressed after savage fighting, commemorated by piled corpses around the bases of two seated statues of the pharaoh found at Nekhen. Khasekhem changed his name to Khasekhemwy, "Appearance of Two Powers" and tactfully caused his serekh to bear the names of both Horus and Seth. He married a northern princess named Nemathap as a gesture toward better relations. A surviving clay jar seal records her title as "the King-bearing Mother." She was the ancestral figure of the 3rd dynasty, when the Egyptian state came of age.

3RD DYNASTY: DJOSER AND IMHOTEP

The greatest of the 3rd dynasty pharaohs was Djoser, whose Horus name was Netjerikhet, "Divine of the Body." Djoser came to the throne in around 2630 B.C. and reigned for 19 years. He had to contend with some political unrest on Egypt's borders, both in the Sinai and upstream from Memphis. He succeeded in extending his rule southward to the First Cataract, which later became the official southern frontier of the kingdom. We do not know if he was a strong ruler, but his vizier was so competent it may not have mattered.

Djoser's vizier, Imhotep, was "Treasurer of the King of Lower Egypt, the First after the King of Upper Egypt, Administrator of the Great Palace, Hereditary Lord, the High Priest of Heliopolis, Imhotep the builder, the sculptor, the maker of stone vases...." Few pharaohs were served by such a remarkable vizier. Imhotep was the son of a famous architect named Kaneferu and the greatest genius of the Old Kingdom. He achieved such fame as a wise court official, architect, scribe, and healer that he was deified by the Egyptians 1,400 years later. His imposing titles appear on a shattered base of a statue of his master. Imhotep was the power behind the throne of a king whose principal fame comes from his architect's achievements.

Imhotep was high priest of the sun god, Re, at Heliopolis, 20 miles north of Memphis. His priests were expert astronomers who had studied the movements of the heavenly bodies over many centuries. They knew how to calculate the passage of time from the rising and setting of the stars; they understood much of the science of geometry and how to use the stars for finding direction. Their sun cult promulgated the legend of the primeval mound, rising from the watery chaos in the shape of the pyramidal stone, the benben, revered in the sanctuary at Heliopolis. As time went on, the teachings of Heliopolis brought together all manner of local religious beliefs, creating

FOLLOWING PAGES: Maidum was the first true pyramid, commissioned by King Snefru in about 2575 B.C. More than 15 years in the building, Maidum originally boasted eight steps and smooth sides. The pyramid either collapsed or was quarried away, leaving the three-step tower of today.

the familiar pantheon of Egyptian gods, headed by the sun god, the heavenly king, Re or Re-Herakhty.

The pharaoh ruled on Earth as Re's representative. Each day Re-Herakhty sailed in his bark over the waters of heaven, bringing light and life to a world that otherwise would be moribund as it was before creation. At sunset Re changed boats and became inert in the form of a ram-headed manifestation of the creator, passing over the waters under Earth. There he battled with the demonic forces of Isfet, led by the snake-god Apophis. Triumphant, the sun god emerged on the sun-bark at the beginning of a new young day as the next cycle of creation began.

Under the new doctrines Djoser was more than a personification of Horus, he ruled on Earth as the son of Re, or even as a manifestation of the sun god himself. He and Imhotep boldly changed the superstructure of his tomb to reflect their innovative theology. The primordial mound now became a stepped pyramid, a stairway whereby the deceased pharaoh could ascend to the sky to join Re in his solar boat at the moment when the rising sun illuminated the summit. At the same time the king ordered his pyramid built not alongside his ancestors at Abydos, but far downstream at Saqqara, in the desert west of Memphis.

With bold confidence Djoser and Imhotep embarked on a vast construction project unlike anything attempted along the Nile before, building in stone for eternity rather than in mud brick. The logistics were overwhelming. Imhotep and his officials had to recruit, transport, feed and house, deploy, and supervise thousands of laborers from villages throughout the land. One large workforce quarried limestone from the cliffs at Tura across the Nile, another shipped the rough blocks across the river to Saqqara, and a third hauled the blocks and installed them under the supervision of expert artisans. All this had to be concentrated into the inundation months, when the fields were idle. At one stroke the state broke down the isolation of hundreds of village communities, mingling them with their fellow countrymen in what must have been seen as a common act of piety, a gesture toward a sacred cosmos—somewhat similar to building a medieval cathedral. The consequences were enormous.

Imhotep created a stunning tribute to immortality. Djoser's six-level Step Pyramid stands in the center of a 912-by-1788-foot enclosure. The base of the lowest level measures 351 feet from north to south and 400 feet from east to west. Egyptologist David O'Connor has argued persuasively that the prototype for the enclosure and

Archaeologists found the looted burial chamber of King Snefru in the Maidum

Pyramid in 1882. A long passage from the pyramid's north face leads to the small

chamber with its corbeled roof. Some of the logs spanning the roof still survive.

This crude, undecorated room would evolve, in time, to become the elaborately

decorated burial chambers of the later pharaohs.

pyramid was the earlier mortuary enclosures at Abydos, but this time more elaborate in plan and made of stone. In this case the symbolic primordial mound of creation was expanded to form the Step Pyramid. Inside the pyramid a maze of subterranean passages attempted to foil tomb robbers, disguising a 92-foot shaft adorned with fine reliefs and blue faience (glazed) tiles that led to Djoser's burial chamber. A three-ton rock plug sealed the granite-lined burial chamber with its 13-foot ceiling. Vast numbers of stone vessels, some bearing the names of earlier kings, have been taken from the passages, vessels that were perhaps offerings by the king to his predecessors. In the end robbers outwitted Imhotep's ingenuity. They stripped the burial chamber and tore the royal mummy apart. Only Djoser's mummified left foot survives. In a cell-like chamber on the north side of the pyramid, a life-size seated figure of the pharaoh, wearing the white cloak worn at the festivals commemorating his rule, gazes out at the stars of the northern sky, the Imperishables that never set.

A thick stone wall with external towers surrounded the Step Pyramid. The builders used a simple version of the now familiar palace facade motif on the outside, adorning it with 211 bastions and 14 great portals, only one a true entrance, for the king's ka, vital force, to pass. The main gateway at the southeastern corner led to an entrance hall 174 feet long, decorated with columns. The hall in turn opened into a vestibule with four pairs of columns shaped to mimic the sway of leafy plants.

On the south side of the enclosure, the so-called South Tomb faced the Step Pyramid. There are many theories concerning its function. Djoser's viscera were probably buried here, in opposition to his mummy under the pyramid, fulfilling the need for a northern and southern sepulchre to match the Two Lands.

Imhotep laid out a Court of Royal Appearance at the foot of the pyramid, which measured 354 by 613 feet, with a replica of a royal palace at the southwestern corner. A pair of stone horseshoe-shaped cairns stood at each end of the plaza, facing an elevated throne dias shaded by a canopy at the foot of the pyramid. The layout of the court and the ceremonies to be performed in it went back deep into history. The Narmer Macehead dating to about 3000 B.C. shows the ruler sitting on a similar canopied dias facing prisoners of war and animals captured in battle, arrayed between boundary markers like those at Saqqara. A wooden label from the tomb of King Den of the 1st dynasty at Abydos shows the king sitting on a canopied dias, a hieroglyphic sign for his reign behind him. Pharaoh Den appears a second time at the foot of the dias, striding between six territorial markers. Similarly two groups of three carved panels in false

At Saqqara the richly
decorated tomb of Ti, who
supervised the pyramids
and temples at nearby
Abusir during the reigns
of the 5th dynasty kings
Neferirkare and Neuserre
(ca 2400 B.C.), achieved
fame in ancient times for
its magnificent scenes
of daily life on his large
estate. In the afterlife
wall decorations such as
this would come alive and
perpetuate the great
wealth Ti had enjoyed
on Earth. His sepulchre
is a mine of information
on the idyllic lives of the
powerful and wealthy
in the Old Kingdom.
Here female servants bring
offerings—a basket of
fruit, a young goat,
bread, and beer.

An Old Kingdom scribe of the 5th dynasty from Saqqara sits in the classic pose

of a high official, wearing the simple white kilt of his class. His left hand unrolls

a papyrus scroll; the other rests on the document—hands that never knew manual

labor. Because scribes could read and write, they garnered great respect in Egypt,

where writing was invented to keep intricate records of production and taxes.

doorways, supposedly for underground passages under the Step Pyramid, show Djoser performing exactly the same ceremony, striding between the symbolic boundaries of his domains. Later inscriptions tell us the cairns were markers of territorial limits placed in what was called "the field."

Egyptian belief held that the pharaoh received understanding from the sun god while still in the womb. The pharaoh was *netjer*, a god. But the pharaoh was of human origin and, thus, required a tomb after death. Unlike the gods, a pharaoh had to observe regular jubilees of revivification to ensure the continued fertility of the land. The Heb-sed festival, one of the greatest ceremonies of state, was performed exactly 30 years after the king's accession—and at more frequent intervals later in the reign. Heb-sed commemorated the earthly power and vigor of the king and always embraced two elements. First the ruler would appear in full regalia and sit on a special dias provided with two thrones, symbolizing the Two Lands. Then he would stride around territorial cairns set in the field, thereby renewing his claim to the kingdom.

Heb-sed and its elaborate pageantry had profound importance in religious life, for it reemphasized the close relationship between the divine king and a unified land. We have few eyewitness accounts of Heb-sed, the best from 1,300 years later when the New Kingdom Pharaoh Amenhotep III celebrated no less than three such ceremonies at Thebes, in the 30th, 34th, and 37th years of his long reign. He even ordered his scribes to research earlier ceremonies, including Djoser's. Instead of striding around an arena, Amenhotep ordered the digging of a large artificial basin measuring a mile by a half-mile where the western Nile floodplain met the desert. A small army of workers spread the soil from the depression to make a terrace for the king's mortuary temple and adjacent palace, landscaped into rows of low hills.

The climax of the first ceremony saw "the glorious appearance of the king at the great double doors in his palace, 'The House of Rejoicing,' ushering in the officials, the king's friends, the chamberlain...and the king's dignitaries." Amenhotep honored high officials with gifts and gave them the privilege of towing the evening and morning barges in the basin. The barges carried statues of the sun god, and towing them reenacted the sun's daily journey.

Djoser's Step Pyramid was an elaborate setting for the display of kingship and of the ruler himself, either to his courtiers or to the populace at large. The setting provided a large open space, an elevated place where the king (Continued on page 86)

To build the Pyramids of
Giza, between 2550 and
2472 B.C., an estimated
20,000 to 30,000 people
labored annually. Royal
architects used the
simplest of surveying
and leveling methods.
Working year-round in
rotation, teams of farmers
from throughout the land
quarried stone and hauled
trimmed blocks and core
rubble up earthen ramps
that wrapped around each
rising pyramid. Artisans
set each load in place,
shaping external masonry
to fit. Pharaoh Khufu
constructed the mightiest
pyramid, yet only a two-
and-a-half-inch-tall ivory
statuette of his physical
form survives (right, top).

Horus, the falcon god of
kings, embraces Pharaoh
Khafre from behind (right,
middle). Two female
deities flank his successor,
Pharaoh Menkaure
(right, bottom).

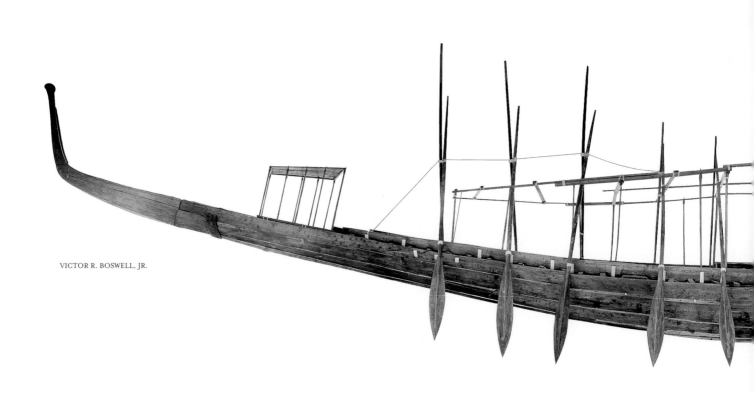

VICTOR R. BOSWELL, JR.

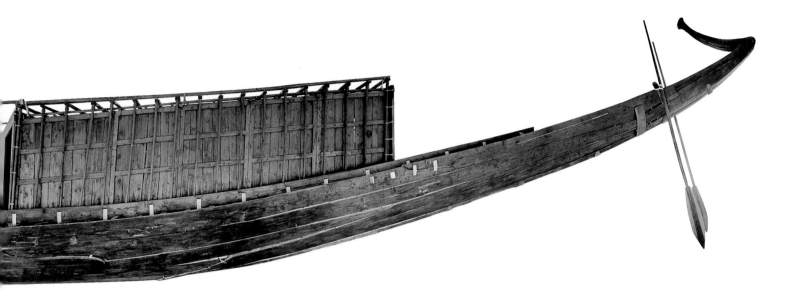

A PORT FOR ETERNITY

Empty boat-shaped pits east of Khufu's Great Pyramid cluster like a dock for the journey to the otherworld. Two of the pits found on the south side contained disassembled craft. Egyptian Ahmed Youssef reassembled one of the cedar boats, 142 feet long, from 1,224 parts, bored with U-shaped holes so they could be stitched together with vegetable fiber (top). The boat, with prow and stern in the form of papyrus stalks and a reed-mat cabin amidships, had been carefully taken apart perhaps for Khufu's symbolic ascent to the heavens. Another disassembled boat lies in a pit to the west, investigated by the Egyptian Antiquities Authority and National Geographic with a periscopic camera inserted through the roof. Inside Khufu's Great Pyramid the grand gallery (left) exhibits masterful corbeled walling, its roof 26 feet high and spanned by stone slabs. In Ti's sepulchre (opposite), a boatbuilding crew shape and assemble a planked Nile boat.

The Giza Pyramids loom on the horizon for all to see, as their royal owners intended. Recent excavations have revealed the elaborate satellite pyramid, causeway, and valley temple associated with Pharaoh Khufu.

could be seen by the crowd, and a token palace where he could rest or change his regalia. But it was all illusion. Djoser never performed the Heb-sed at Saqqara. But his pyramid and court of appearance on Earth would come into use in the afterlife.

PYRAMIDS: THE MOUNTAINS OF RE

The Egyptians' funerary traditions permeated every aspect of daily life—the growing of food and recording of harvests, art and architecture, trade and transportation, and writing. For five centuries Old Kingdom kings lavished most of their country's manpower and wealth on building tombs and mortuary temples to ensure their immortality. Pyramid construction and an obsession with the afterlife created a unified state in a way that no pharaoh could have done on his own.

Djoser's successors embarked on a frenzy of pyramid building at the edge of the desert, in places where the summer inundation allowed stone-laden barges to come. The largest pyramids were erected between 2575 and 2494 B.C. by three generations of 4th dynasty pharaohs—Snefru, his son Khufu, and grandson Khafre.

When Snefru came to the throne in 2575 B.C., he completed an eight-step pyramid in stages at Maidum, 35 miles south of Saqqara, then abruptly moved his necropolis 25 miles north to Dahshur. He may have wanted a site closer to the delta, where royal monopolies on the cedar trade from the Levant and other commercial activities required attention. Snefru commissioned two pyramids at Dahshur as his architects experimented with the true, smooth pyramid shape. Their first attempt ran into problems of settling, resulting in a bent profile. They learned from their mistakes and built Snefru's Red Pyramid at a gentler angle of 43 degrees, achieving a simple and elegant structure. After all this effort Snefru sent his tomb-builders back to Maidum and instructed them to transform the steps into a true pyramid shape of 51° 50' 35". The architects duly filled three steps, but the work ceased when Snefru died. No one knows where he was buried—perhaps under the Red Pyramid or even in a sarcophagus of Aswan red granite found in an inconspicuous tomb close to the empty Maidum Pyramid. Unfortunately the carefully bandaged human bones in the red sarcophagus were shipped to the British Museum in 1910 and lost, so the mystery remains unsolved.

Snefru may have been a demanding taskmaster, but a much later papyrus depicts him as a kindly monarch. Prince Bauefre, a son of Pharaoh Khufu, recalled a day when Snefru, his grandfather, was wandering bored through his palace. He summoned the

chief priest Djadja-em-ankh, who suggested an outing on the nearby lake in a boat rowed by "all the beauties which are in the palace chamber." Snefru was delighted. "Let there be brought to me 20 nets, and let these nets be given to the women when they have taken off their clothes.... And the heart of His Majesty was happy at this sight of their rowing"—and, presumably, at their see-through fishnet costumes.

Snefru's son Khufu moved northward to the Giza plateau near modern-day Cairo. Here his architects, using surveying equipment no more complex than long strings, plumb bobs, sighting poles, and other simple architects' and masons' tools, laid out a stupendous pyramid with its sides oriented almost exactly to true north. Then Khufu built one of the largest stone structures ever erected anywhere as part of a spectacular mortuary complex without rival.

The Great Pyramid, known as Akhet Khufu, "the Horizon of Khufu," towers 451 feet above the Giza plateau and probably contains about 2.3 million stone blocks, weighing on average about 2.5 tons. The builders worked with astounding accuracy: The base is level to within less than an inch, the orientation only 3' 6" off cardinal north. Perhaps to avoid problems like those at Dahshur, they founded the outer casing on a specially leveled platform constructed on bedrock and used good quality limestone for the corners and upper courses. The entire pyramid was encased in white Tura limestone, much of which was stripped off centuries later to build the Islamic citadel in medieval Cairo. A system of galleries and passageways led to a red-granite burial chamber where the king's mummy lay in a sarcophagus of the same material. A causeway connected the Great Pyramid to a valley temple at the edge of a rock-cut harbor leading to the Nile. Khufu's burial complex even included dismantled boats in special pits, which may have carried the body to the valley temple or may have functioned as solar boats for the king in the afterlife.

Finally Khufu authorized the creation of cemeteries of rock-cut tombs near his pyramid—to the east for royal relatives and to the west for his high officials.

Not to be outdone, Khufu's son Khafre built his pyramid complex immediately southwest of his father's. He aligned it along a diagonal that pointed northeast in the direction of Heliopolis, the home of the benben, and southwest toward Abydos. His pyramid is smaller than Khufu's, rising to 471 feet, but built on bedrock some 33 feet higher. He compensated for his smaller burial place with a large mortuary temple linked by causeway to a valley temple built of stone blocks sheathed in red granite. A dim T-shaped hall, lit only by narrow slits in the walls just below the ceiling, held 24 statues of Khafre set in pits along the walls. The king's body may have been embalmed here.

Khafre seems to have loved seeing himself depicted in stone. Statues of him abound, the largest being the Sphinx, which represents the king as Horus, a colossal sculpture of a human-headed lion carved from the natural bedrock at the base of the causeway. The lion was a solar symbol in ancient Egypt, the royal head emblematic of the power and authority embodied by the pharaoh, and a symbol of ma'at and cosmic order. The head wears the *nemes* headdress folded in a way associated only with kings, its flaring sides forming the lion's mane. Sphinxes remained a part of Egyptian iconography for more than 2,500 years.

Khafre's successor, Menkaure, reigned for 20 years or more and apparently left his pyramid complex unfinished. The sepulchre lies at the far end of the Giza plateau where less space was available. The resulting pyramid has about a tenth the mass of the Great Pyramid. As the burial place shrank, the mortuary temple grew. A larger-than-life statue of Menkaure stood at the back of the temple with a clear view down the pyramid causeway toward the Nile and the land of the living. A false door behind the statue let the dead king receive offerings and project his vital force across the land.

FOLLOWING PAGES: Queen Meresankh III, Khufu's granddaughter and wife of Khafre, was buried in a sculpted and painted rock-cut tomb in the eastern cemetery at Giza. Prepared for her by her mother, the sepulchre attests to the power and independence enjoyed by some women of means in ancient Egypt.

Why did the pharaohs construct such enormous burial places? Perhaps their motives were strictly religious, the pyramids being cosmic engines that ensured a continuity of order in a world of chaos—the rising and setting of the sun, the annual inundations of Nile waters. The pyramid was where life and light and death and darkness met. The pharaoh ruled as a living god. At death his divine manifestation, *ba,* and vital force, *ka,* left his body. Before his mummy was laid to rest under the pyramid, it was stood upright outside the entrance and purified with incense and water. Then the high priest twice raised an adzelike implement to the face of the mummy and its ka statue. He also touched it with a forked wand, which magically restored the bodily senses of the deceased ruler. At this moment the pharaoh's ba and ka rejoined the body. His ka was rooted to the tomb and received sustenance for the deceased. The imperishable ba could travel in and out of the tomb—between the earthly and divine realms. When the ba traveled to the divine realm and became immortal, it could join the ranks of imperishable *akhs,* or transfigured spirits. The kings' akhs resided in a divine celestial realm where, if "well equipped," they had potent magical powers to assist the deceased and affect those on Earth for good or ill.

The pharaohs' motives may also have been political. In Snefru's time Egypt was still a loose-knit patchwork of nomes, each loyal to local leaders and a myriad of small-time deities. The court culture of the pharaohs was remote from the humble villages of the countryside. Some Egyptologists believe that the construction of the pyramids demanded new thinking, where the powerful king reached out to the remotest villages for food, labor, and raw materials of all kinds. Royal officials and scribes drew tight the reins of centralized government and organized the state as they had previously organized the imperial armies and trading expeditions. Pyramid building defined not only the frontier between life and death but also the power of the pharaoh as provider. The state must have provided on a huge scale. Many Egyptologists believe that 20,000 to 30,000 people worked intensively on pyramid construction for the three months of the agricultural year when the Nile inundated the land. Skilled builders and artisans probably worked at the site year-round, but their numbers are undetermined.

We know from inscriptions on the stones that most of the workforce was made up of groups of village conscript laborers numbering about 2,000 and divided into two gangs of 1,000 each. Each gang was divided into five *zaa* of 200 workers (often called *phyles,* after the Greek word for "tribe"), each zaa comprising ten teams of 20 men. The gangs had names like "Drunkards of Menkaure," while each phyle possessed

a standard name, such as "Great," "Asiatic," "Green," "Little," and "Last."

Money was unknown in ancient Egypt, so the language of all economic activity was commodities, especially food. Loaves of bread, jugs of beer, measures of wheat, dried fish—these and many other goods formed the currency of Egypt in which the pyramid workforce was paid. Everyone, from the architect to the lowliest manual laborer, received food as wages. The state supervised the growing and manufacture of foodstuffs, stock raising, and fishing, from the moment of inception until the moment that rations were distributed. Records tell us that the basic standard daily wage for a laborer consisted of ten loaves and a measure of beer that could range between a third of a jug to one or two full ones. Rations increased by multiples of the basic ration to the point where an entitlement far exceeded an individual and his family's collective appetite. Much of the surplus food wage must have been distributed in some form of credit system, exchangeable for textiles, ornaments, and other minor luxuries.

The supervision of construction consumed many hours of scribal time, scrutinizing and measuring precise quantities of raw materials, even ensuring that each laborer carried, transported, or dug his proper day's work for the rations he received. For example, ten cubic cubits (a cubit is about 20 inches) was the daily norm for a man transporting raw materials. The scribe's pen was as much a driving force behind construction as the ingenuity of the king's engineers or the supervisors who kept the labor gangs working.

Quite apart from the construction of the pyramid complexes, small armies of priests and workers labored to fulfill the dead pharaoh's needs in the afterlife. New villages and estates were founded near Giza to service the needs of the pyramids and their royal cults. The remains of a substantial town settlement lies south-southeast of the pyramids, detected during construction work to install a modern sewage system. A massive stone wall 33 feet high, with a 23-foot gateway, separated the sacred precincts around the pyramid complex from the secular activities without. Only a small part of the town has been excavated so far, part of a vast royal complex that seems to have housed production facilities, workers, and their supervisors. The excavators have uncovered two large galleries, separated by a paved street 17 feet wide. Each contains bakeries and copper workshops, also small workers' dwellings, partially protected from the sun by a roof supported on a massive colonnade. Two buildings, one at each end, controlled access into what must have been a large, closely supervised manufacturing area. As part of an earlier excavation, Egyptologist Mark Lehner excavated a bakery, which turned out thousands of standard-size loaves, and a fish-processing-and-drying facility—rations for pyramid workers.

FOLLOWING PAGES: Partially buried, a stone wall known as the Wall of the Crow once separated the workers' town from the royal necropolis. Workers passed through the gateway in the morning to work on the pyramid and in the evening to receive rations. Behind the wall crouches the Sphinx, built about 2500 B.C. for King Khafre. New Kingdom pharaohs worshiped the pharaoh-headed lion as a symbol of divinity.

Near the galleries, to the west, an Egyptian team found two cemeteries. The lower cemetery was used for the burial of the workmen who moved the stones; the upper one was used for the artisans.

Egyptian archaeologist and field director of the excavation Zahi Hawass dug the tomb of a man named Nefer-thieth, who had 2 wives and 18 children. His second wife, Nyankh-Hathor, was a midwife. Nefer-thieth's occupation is unknown, but he may have been a bakery or brewery supervisor, for many scenes in the tomb depict bread- and beer-making. Hawass has excavated more than 600 pyramid workers' tombs, most less than a few feet square. None of the workers was mummified, at that time still a privilege reserved for the elite, but their bones tell of harsh lives of unremitting toil. Arthritis and degenerative spinal problems from backbreaking labor were common-place. Most of the laborers died young.

RULERS AND THE RULED

We know almost nothing about the three Giza kings. The gossipy Herodotus paints an unflattering portrait of Khufu, who, he says, reduced the country "to a completely awful condition" and drafted all his countrymen to work on his pyramid. He was told that they worked in gangs of 100,000 men for three months at a time. "There is a notice in Egyptian script on the pyramid about how much was spent on radishes, onions, and garlic for the laborers, and if my memory serves me well, the translator reading the notice to me said that the total cost was 1,600 talents of silver." Herodotus also claimed that the despotic Khufu made his daughter sell her favors to pay for his tomb. His son Khafre was as bad: "The Egyptians loathe Chephren [Khafre] and Cheops [Khufu] so much that they really do not like to mention their names." Menkaure was a fairer ruler, who ended much of the tyranny.

The 4th dynasty pharaohs have passed into history as despots, but they remain surprisingly anonymous. Khufu built the greatest pyramid of all, but only one small ivory statuette of the king survives. Khafre and Menkaure are better known, depicted as calm, well-muscled rulers, men of physical strength and confident authority. All three of them must have been leaders of remarkable ability and charisma. Their pyramids may have been erected as acts of faith by a loyal populace, but to channel this loyalty into logistical reality took an army of efficient administrators, artisans, and scribes.

What manner of men supervised the kingdom and the construction of the Giza

Khufu's pyramid shadows the tombs of his queens and nobles buried in the eastern cemetery. Only the highest officials and royal relatives enjoyed the privilege of burial within sight of the pharaoh's pyramid. The carvings, paintings, and statuary of these rock-cut tombs hold a wealth of information on the daily lives of the wealthy and well-stationed few during the height of the Old Kingdom.

pyramids? We know of them from their statues and tomb paintings. The conventions of Old Kingdom art depict them with a serene naturalism that does not disguise their competence and ability. Many came from close-knit noble families who married among each other and inherited high office from their fathers.

Hemiunu, a grandson of King Snefru, was overseer of all construction projects for Khufu. His seated statue, once painted red with inlaid eyes and eyelashes of gold, is large and obese, but the unflattering portrait does not disguise the charisma of the man. He must have been a forceful character of boundless energy to erect the Great Pyramid in a mere 23 years of his master's reign. His titles inscribed on his statue say it all: "Member of the elite, high official, vizier, king's seal-bearer...Director of Music of the South and North, Overseer of All Construction."

Hemiunu and his ilk stood at the very pinnacle of Egypt's social pyramid. They enjoyed the pharaoh's confidence and carried out his wishes. Titles assumed great importance in a society where rank was often hereditary and the favor of the king counted for everything. Not that the life at court was easy. The pharaoh and his courtiers lived a rarified existence of lavish banquets and magnificent dress, where the formal protocol surrounding the king dictated the routine of every day. A choreographed existence certainly, but one fraught with tension and intense personal rivalries. The king presided over a state that was a patchwork of nomes, each ruled by a powerful governor, loyal to the pharaoh but always alert for signs of weakness in Memphis. In about 2180 B.C. drought made the central government helpless, and the southern governors became rulers of their local domains. Every pharaoh had several wives and often numerous children, creating a family dynamic in which different branches maneuvered for position or even plotted against the king.

The thorny issue of succession was always at the back of people's minds in a time when life expectancy was short and kings and their sons might die suddenly. The succession passed nominally from father to eldest son by the ruler's chief queen. When such a child was lacking or died prematurely, a child of a junior wife would be elevated to crown prince. The pharaoh would proclaim his successor in public, a routine matter when the eldest son still lived, but a matter of intrigue and jockeying for position when a new heir had to be nominated or when no son survived at all. If there were no sons, very often a senior political or military figure would be nominated, especially if he had royal blood in his veins. Since the rulers were divine, with all the potential for possessing supernatural powers which that entailed, having a royal blood relationship

was clearly desirable. Some pharaohs appointed their sons as co-regents while they were still active, a wise precaution in an era when all royal sons received training in kingship, just in case they came unexpectedly to the throne. A strong pharaoh like Khufu or Khafre kept these potentially disruptive forces in check, while a weak ruler had to appease the competing interests of his powerful subordinates. Divine kings they might be, but in a world where they were considered infallible, an indecisive ruler did not reign long.

The king would grant some of his high officials the right to use the services of royal artisans for their mortuary statues and tombs. The priest Memi wears a curly wig and spotless white kilt. One of the two inscriptions on his seated statue proclaims: *"Wab* priest of the king, Memi, who walks on the beautiful paths on which the honored walk." The sculptors often crafted officials sitting in pairs—devoted husband and wife clasping one another, the relationship between them being expressed by gestures and subtle poses. Even mid-level officials commissioned sculptures of themselves seated, like Inti-Shedu, "Overseer of the Boat of [the goddess] Neith," who gained immortality by an accident of preservation. His efforts at self-aggrandizement survived the millennia for archaeologists to find.

The paintings and reliefs in the elite's imposing tombs (*Continued on page 104*)

PYRAMID BUILDING

Thousands of anonymous—skilled and unskilled—
workers built the pyramids. Like his remote ancestors
a crew member from a Nile cargo boat (above)
unloads construction stone destined for Cairo.
Ancient Egyptians hefted small stones like this one
for Djoser's Step Pyramid, and teams of workers
moved blocks weighing up to 15 tons with sledges
and rollers at Giza. A nearby town (right) housed the
artisans, priests, scribes, laborers, and their families.
Adjacent cemeteries excavated by Egyptologist Zahi
Hawass contain the tombs of thousands of workers
and artisans in tiny graves grouped near the larger
tombs of their masters. The men who built the pyramids ranked as the pharaohs' finest craftsmen, not
slaves of the state, as previously thought. Today the
pyramids still soar as symbols not only of the divine
pharaohs who ruled ancient Egypt but also of human
ingenuity and skillfulness in craftsmanship.

THEIR DAILY BREAD

Bread built the pyramids. Thousands of workers lived off carefully apportioned rations—loaves of emmer wheat and dried fish, with beer to drink. Large industrial-scale bakeries in the workers' towns turned out thousands of standard-size loaves a week from grain winnowed by hand (left). Pyramid expert Mark Lehner has excavated a pyramid town bakery dating to the time of Pharaoh Menkaure. Lehner and ancient-bread expert Edward Wood, with National Geographic support, built a replica of the bakery and commissioned copies of Egyptian bread pots from a Cairo potter. Using native yeast spores and bacteria as rising agents, they poured the dough into pot bottoms, then set them in hot coals to rise (above). Preheated pot tops placed over the bottom halves created an oven effect. An hour and 40 minutes later Wood enjoyed slices from perfect loaves. In ancient Egypt each loaf fed a large family, hefted from bakery to home on a man's shoulder, a scene oft repeated in stone reliefs.

LOAVES AND FISHES

Scrape, scrape—the sound of grinder against milling
stone was everywhere in ancient Egypt. Every working
woman spent hours a day on her knees preparing
grain to make bread or beer (above). X-ray analysis
of back, arm, and toe bones shows the inevitable
stress of constant kneeling and pushing, resulting
in osteoarthritis even among relatively young women.
The wheat-based diet included fish, a source of protein
still popular today as indicated by Cairo's fish market
(right). A huge mud-brick building in the Giza pyramid
town has yielded gills, fins, and other small fragments
of catfish and Nile schal. The soil on the building's
shelves contained tiny broken fish bones. Catfish breed
soon after the Nile's annual inundation, so fishermen
would fan out along the river and catch thousands.
The catch was gutted, dried, and perhaps smoked
or salted to make rations for hungry workers.

near the pyramids tell us much about their lives on country estates granted them by the king. Teams of men with enormous nets snare migrating geese in marshes; farm workers force-feed cranes destined for the pot. In one relief a naked boy chases after a basket of fruit and vegetables at a market as a baboon grasps his right leg. "The Keeper of Baboons Hemu" restrains the animal with a leash and stick, as the boy exclaims, "Hey! Help! Strike in order to scare off this baboon!"

In another sepulchre a herd of cattle wade through a canal. The herdsman carries a calf on his back to encourage the mother cow to follow him. On the right a group of fishermen haul in a net bursting with mullet and other fish. The idealistic tomb scenes are bustling, often emotive, and startlingly realistic—geese squawking, a cow drinking water, men struggling with heavy loads. They present an illusion of the ideal life where the privileged enjoyed luxuries of every kind, served by the anonymous labors of innumerable commoners. One vizier even commissioned a frieze of bare-breasted harem girls, with their weighted pigtails and kicking arms and legs dancing in honor of Hathor, the goddess of fertility. Everyone lived in hope of eternal youth and happiness in the afterlife.

"Know your helpers, then you prosper," the vizier Ptah-hotep instructed his son, as he urged him to be generous and steadfast to his friends. But there was little generosity in a state where the majority served the few and society revolved around a divine king.

Although there was no middle class in Old Kingdom society, a sizable group of artisans, scribes, priests, and petty officials lived off their skills rather than by manual labor. They were the junior officers and sergeants of Egypt's enormous civilian army, the people who furnished estates, palaces, and tombs; wove fine raiment and crafted regalia; commanded regiments in battle; performed temple rituals; and measured crops. Egypt's organized oasis ran smoothly because of this "white kilt" class, who watched everything and everyone, provided manpower, and issued rations.

Under the white kilt class was the vast mass of commoners, taxed and often harassed by petty officialdom, at the mercy of the minor corruption that pervaded society. Theirs was a life of ceaseless, usually repetitive, toil, epitomized by a relief from an Old Kingdom tomb showing a team of donkeys threshing grain. Behind them stands a weary man with weathered face steering the team in their endless rotation. Another frieze shows tax delinquents being hauled before a court. The life of the peasant revolved around the perpetual cycle of the seasons of inundation, planting, and harvest. Compared with the lot of commoners elsewhere, the Egyptian farmer had it easy—in times of abundant flood—because of the richness of the soil and a minimal need for plowing and because of canals and large-scale irrigation. But they still toiled very hard. Even in good times villagers worked from dawn to dusk. Between planting and harvest they labored in the fields at the mercy of the river, digging irrigation canals to protect and enlarge natural flood basins, shoring up dikes, watering their crops—back-breaking work under the best of circumstances. All the irrigation was done by hand, water carried in twin wooden buckets slung on a yoke across naked shoulders. Oxen dragged simple wooden plows over the dark soil, followed by teams of sowers scattering emmer grain from shallow baskets. Here the reality was the flood—not only years of plenty but also the inevitable dreaded years of hunger and dearth when the Nile barely rose above its banks.

The farmers lived in crowded, dusty villages, their garbage piling up in the alleyways between small mud-brick houses. Here women would barter vegetables for fish and minor luxuries. During the high-water season the men labored for the state. Service appears to have been compulsory: Those who ran away were punished. Judging from a surviving Middle Kingdom document, a man's family may have been cast into prison until he gave himself up. Life expectancy was short, clothing minimal—little more than a loincloth for men and perhaps a long, sheath-like dress for women, usually with a high waistline and a V-neck.

The pharaohs presided over a state where most people lived brief lives, suffering was constant, and unquestioning obedience the only way to survive. Old Kingdom Egypt was no idyllic society, except for a privileged few, who gaze out at us with the kind of calm assurance that comes only from hereditary wealth and a complete confidence in one's place in society. They lived off the monotonous labor of others.

RESURRECTION AND ETERNITY

The Pyramids of Giza were a high point. No later pharaoh ever attempted a tomb on such a grandiose scale. Perhaps their expenditures nearly beggared the kingdom. Judging by the smaller size of his pyramid, Menkaure may have been the first to feel the pinch. Later Old Kingdom pharaohs scaled down their pyramids even more and built elaborate mortuary temples instead. Many of the 5th dynasty pharaohs built their smaller pyramid complexes at Abusir, south of Giza, in a northern extension of the Saqqara necropolis.

King Neferefre (ca 2448-2445 B.C.) reigned for little more than two years and died before he was 25. At the time of his death only the base of his unpretentious pyramid was in place. His successor, Neuserre, hastily turned the structure into a gravel-covered low mound and added a mud-brick mortuary temple. One would have thought that the short-lived pharaoh would have been soon forgotten, but he was not. Czech Egyptologist Miroslav Verner has spent many years working at Abusir, using subsurface detection equipment to study Neferefre's mortuary temple. A mud-brick storeroom inside the temple has yielded a cache of more than 2,000 papyrus fragments. These Abusir papyri provide a fascinating chronicle of the minute details of a royal mortuary cult still active more than a century after Neferefre's death.

A permanent staff of priests and scribes, "servants of the god," ran the temple, augmented by local townsfolk as a temporary priesthood. Each served for one month in ten, thereby rotating the duty and privilege of serving the deceased pharaoh. The permanent staff performed the daily rituals, maintained and stocked the temple, carried out essential maintenance, and kept inventory.

Every day the cult priests would circle the pyramid three times in solemn procession. Others would gather in front of a statue of the pharaoh, remove its covering, then sprinkle it with perfume and add eye shadow and other cosmetics. Swinging an incense burner and chanting, they would drape the statue anew in fresh bright fabrics. Meanwhile another priest supervised the food and drink offerings at the temple altar—loaves of bread in different shapes, all specified in a temple papyrus and checked off by a scribe. The offerings lay on the altar long enough for the pharaoh's ka to receive nourishment and were then removed.

The Sanctuary of the Knife was a room in the temple devoted entirely to bull sacrifices. The priests hobbled the sacrificial bulls, then tethered them to great limestone blocks set in the floor. A butcher slit their throats, collecting the blood in a special alabaster basin. The temple papyri tell us that as many as 130 bulls could be sacrificed in the course of a single 10-day festival, a remarkable number for such a short-lived ruler as Neferefre.

Another 5th dynasty pharaoh, Unas, died about 2345 B.C. after a reign of 30 years. He was buried under a rubble core pyramid with smooth limestone casing just south of Djoser's mortuary complex at Saqqara. At his funeral the royal priests chanted the incantations that would help the soul of the king on its journey. Unas broke with long-established tradition, ordering that his burial chamber be adorned with the same spells. Here, as the mummy of Unas lay in the *duat*, the netherworld, his ba awakened and released

FOLLOWING PAGES: Friezes in the causeway that links King Unas's mortuary and valley temples depict emaciated men and women, some with girdles, others naked. They may represent hungry Bedouin nomads who sought refuge in the Nile Valley. Citing recent evidence, some scholars say the friezes may show desert dwellers seen during the Egyptians' expeditions through the desert to quarry stone for Unas's pyramid.

itself from the body. Then it flew into an antechamber (symbolizing the *akhet,* or region between duat and the morning sky), then away through a sky door toward the sunrise and into eternity.

Unas installed white alabaster slabs in his burial place, incised and painted like the matting of a temporary ritual purification tent open to the heavens. The ceiling was adorned with golden stars shining in a deep blue sky. The slabs bear what the Egyptologists call the Pyramid Texts, sacred spells and ritual incantations drawn from what must have been an enormous body of sacred knowledge. The spells protect the pharaoh against snakes and insects. Some list the food, drink, and clothing needed in eternity. There are hymns to the gods and the incantations (complete with instructions for their enactment and delivery) performed at the funeral and in the mortuary temple. The Pyramid Texts mapped out Unas's journey into the afterlife, past all the known obstacles into the heavens where the gods celebrate his homecoming. Unas himself may have arranged the texts in such a way that, should the rituals in his temple break down, he could then rise from his sarcophagus and follow the spells out with the sunrise, thereby transforming himself into an immortal spirit. The king joined the stars, welcomed by the sky goddess Nut:

> *Make your seat in heaven, / Among the stars of heaven, / For you are the Lone Star, the comrade of Hu! / You shall look down on Osiris, / As he commands the spirits....*

After Unas, pyramid texts became a regular feature of the pyramids of kings and queens of the 6th dynasty. About 2184 B.C. the 6th dynasty Pharaoh Pepi I's pyramid texts cleared the way for the ascent to heaven: "Hail to you ladder of the God!...Stand up, Ladder of Horus, which was made for Osiris that he might ascend on it to the sky...Now let the ladder of the God be given to me." Pyramids, mortuary temples, and their accompanying texts in green-painted hieroglyphs, the color of rebirth, were part of a complex resurrection machine that endured as long as Egyptian civilization itself.

SETTING THE FEAR OF HORUS

Few documents recount the historical events of the Old Kingdom. All we know are the names of the pharaohs and some of their spectacular monuments. We know that they spent much time maintaining political order, keeping a watchful eye on overly ambitious nomarchs, and protecting Egypt's frontiers. As time went on

French Egyptologist Audran Labrousse studies the restored pyramid texts

at the entrance to King Pepi I's burial chamber. One of the passages proclaims:

"Stand up, Ladder of Horus, which was made for Osiris that he might ascend

on it to the sky.... Now let the ladder of the God be given to me."

and the state grew larger and more complex, the old network of nobility and close kin gave way to a government run by trusted commoners. During the 4th dynasty the pharaohs had closed off high administrative ranks from royal relatives and entrusted them, instead, to individuals of lower birth; some became known as "king's sons." A vizier or chief minister, sometimes a single individual, occasionally two ministers, administered the country and presided over government: bureaucracies that handled granaries and the treasury, public works, the judiciary, and the civil service. High government officials were rotated around the country according to need, ability, and royal command.

By the 5th dynasty some Upper Egyptian families became heavily entrenched in provincial government and served as hereditary nomarchs. In the long term this led to an effective decentralization of government as these officials took on the airs of royalty and sometimes referred to themselves as "great chiefs." They became a hereditary provincial nobility and a strong counterbalance to the power of the pharaoh.

The ruler's second major concern was foreign policy. Egypt was well protected from the outside world by virtually impassable deserts, the sea, and the Nile cataracts. Foreigners could enter the country at relatively few points, and they normally did so on the pharaoh's terms. The world outside was a domain of chaos. Across the Sinai Desert lay *Setjet*, "the northern lands" of the Asiatics. Miners, traders, and royal couriers passed this way along routes memorized by their stopping places, the forerunners of the camel caravan routes of later times. Egypt's main commercial interests lay to the north, where good ports like Byblos, now in Lebanon, had direct access to cedar and other fine woods, a cherished royal monopoly throughout the Old Kingdom. Here too the pharaoh's traders could connect with middlemen from the city of Ebla in modern-day Syria, which handled Mesopotamian goods. Ebla provided abundant supplies of silver and lapis lazuli, as well as a secure trading environment.

The Egyptians had a profound contempt for "vile Asiatics," whom they considered "the abomination of Re," but they could not prevent them from settling in the delta. Even before unification Canaanites flocked to Egypt in search of work in a fertile land far more bountiful than their own. Many such immigrants became important and wealthy members of Egyptian society and even intermarried with the nobility. Many of Egypt's best winemakers were Syrians, who settled in the delta.

Pharaoh after pharaoh waged war to secure the Asian frontier. The much honored official, Weni, commanded an army for Pepi I against "the Asiatic Sand-dwellers" of the east. "His majesty made an army of many tens of thousands from all of Upper

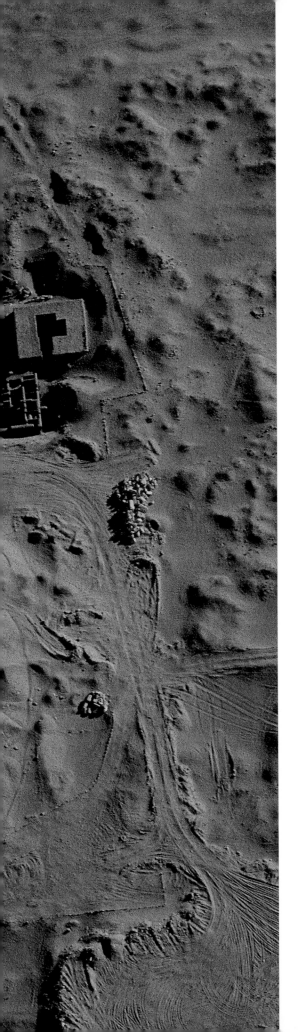

KINGDOM IN DECAY

The 34-year reign of Pharaoh Pepi I (ca 2289-2255 B.C.) saw Old Kingdom Egypt go into slow decline. Royal control weakened; ambitious provincial governors usurped powers. The white limestone and obsidian eyes of a life-size copper statue of Pepi I flash brightly over the millennia (above). Despite the deteriorating political situation, Pepi spent lavishly on his town and pyramid complex, *Men-nefer Pepi,* "The Perfection of Pepi is Established." Pepi's pyramid, now a low mound, once stood 172 feet high and 258 feet on each side. The French Archaeological Saqqara Mission, using electromagnetic sounding equipment in and around the pyramid (left), have uncovered five queens' pyramids, one belonging to Nebwenet, another to Inenek/Inti, a third to Merytytyes, a daughter as well as a royal wife.

Egypt...; from Lower Egypt.... I was the one who commanded them.... This army returned in safety, / It had ravaged the Sand-dwellers' land. . . ."

Above the First Cataract lay Nubia, a desert land to be exploited and later colonized. Nubian specialist William Adams once aptly remarked that "for millennia Egypt treated [Nubia] as a kind of private game reserve for human and animal game." Nubia straddled the middle Nile, a narrow strip of fertile land that extended upstream into modern-day Sudan as far as the borders of Ethiopia. The most fertile valley lands were along the Dongola Reach between the Third and Fourth Cataracts where powerful African states were to develop in later times.

As early as 3000 B.C. the shadow of Egypt began to fall over Nubia. Old Kingdom pharaohs assembled large armies and marched them south to subdue a land rich in resources. Their generals returned with plentiful prisoners and many head of cattle. The process was called "setting the fear of Horus [the pharaoh] among the southern foreign lands, to pacify [them]." Many campaigns were little more than slave raids, which brought back as many as several thousand captives and depopulated northern Nubia. One 4th dynasty graffito refers to as many as 17,000 Nubian prisoners-of-war. Once in Egypt they were set to work on the land or on construction projects and enrolled in the military. In later centuries Nubian mercenaries formed a major element in pharaonic armies. Carefully organized prospecting expeditions brought back to Egypt other rich resources besides humans: gold, ebony, ivory, incense, myrrh, animal skins, and semiprecious stones.

Harkhuf, a 6th dynasty governor of Upper Egypt, led no fewer than four trading expeditions into Nubia. His trips southward took him not up the Nile, but along the so-called Oasis Road. The overland route led from Middle Egypt through a chain of four desert oases before regaining the Nile Valley at Tushka, in Nubia. Harkhuf and his parties traveled on hundreds of donkeys, which enabled him to complete one successful journey in seven months and to travel on other occasions deep into Nubia to the kingdom of Yam, which was centered on the town of Kerma south of the Second Cataract. He exchanged gifts with the ruler of Yam and returned with "300 donkeys laden with incense, ebony...elephant tusks, throw sticks, and all sorts of good products." His entourage also included a dancing dwarf. Harkhuf had sent a courier ahead to the court reporting on his doings. The youthful Pharaoh Pepi II wrote back in his own hand in great excitement: "Come north to the residence at once! Hurry and bring with you this pygmy whom you brought from the land of the horizon-dwellers live,

FOLLOWING PAGES: French excavations at a late Old Kingdom site in the Dakhla

Oasis west of the Nile reveal substantial settlements. Provincial rulers had begun

to erect important mortuary monuments with royal approval. Dakhla's imposing

structures proved symptomatic of the dilution of pharaonic power.

hale, and healthy, for the dances of the god, to gladden the heart...."

The Old Kingdom pharaohs treated Nubia and its people with disdain, their lands as places to be exploited, but they never attempted conquest or colonization above the First Cataract. Nevertheless, Egypt's relationship with Nubia and the African lands was much closer than that with the Levant and Asia, especially when extensive gold deposits were discovered in the south during the Middle Kingdom.

THE STOREHOUSE IS EMPTY

Some centuries after the end of the Old Kingdom, a wise man named Ipuwer wrote, "The land is deprived of kingship by a few people who ignore custom." Even in his day, memories of the collapse of the once powerful kingdom were raw and were weighted with lessons for the future. After hundreds of years of excellent floods and plentiful food supplies, the crisis that enveloped Egypt in about 2180 B.C. came as a rude shock. Disdain of foreigners was all very well, but Egypt was paying the price of extravagance. The colossal expense of mortuary complexes, not only for rulers but also for their relatives and high officials, strained the resources of the state's centralized economy. Temple endowments shrank, construction costs were slashed, and public works were curtailed. But the pharaohs still ruled as living, infallible gods.

Pharaoh Pepi II, he of the dwarf, came to the throne in about 2278 B.C. at the age of six. He ruled for either 64 or 94 years (some confusion surrounds his scribe's accuracy), possibly the longest reign in Egyptian history. His kingdom was powerful and perhaps a little complacent. The court at Memphis enjoyed the fruits of long-held royal monopolies over the cedar trade with Byblos and the trade in ivory and other tropical products with Nubia. But Pepi presided over troubled times. Thirty years into Pepi's reign, a Mesopotamian king, perhaps the famous Sargon of Babylon, sacked Byblos and destroyed a major source of Egyptian wealth at one stroke.

The setback came at a bad time. Pepi II was spending large sums on foreign expeditions and worrying about the political ambitions of his nomarchs. The annual inundation faltered, as much drier conditions settled over the eastern Mediterranean world. There were food shortages and signs of political unrest.

During Pepi's predecessors' reigns the nomarchs had become increasingly powerful hereditary officials, protective of their autonomy and even aping the king with their lavish tombs, which no longer lay in the royal necropolis but close to their

centers of power. Pepi attempted to appease them with lavish gifts and honors. As long as the pharaoh offered strong leadership, his spiritual and political authority carried the day. The nomarchs paid their tribute on time and trimmed their sails to the political wind. In the early days of his reign Pepi remained in decisive control. But as he grew older, he became increasingly detached from the day-to-day business of government. The nomarchs became bolder, more powerful, and less respectful.

As Pepi lay dying, catastrophic droughts brought hunger and disease. The court was powerless to prevent famine. With little warning the central government collapsed. The fragile unity of Lower and Upper Egypt fell apart. The royal succession dissolved in chaos. Manetho writes of 70 kings who reigned for 70 days, a chronicle more symbolic of chaos than actuality. A revolving door of weak pharaohs ruled from Memphis, but their domains extended only a few miles from the capital. Old Kingdom Egypt dissolved into a fracture zone of ancient nomes, while invaders from Asia violated the delta. A once prosperous land became a cockpit of warlords and nomarchs, whose loyalties lay with their own people, not with the state.

The lord Ankhtifi became nomarch of Hierakonpolis and Edfu in Upper Egypt just as low floods beset his districts in about 2150 B.C. An ambitious man, Ankhtifi

Pepi II's simple mud-brick pyramid did not compare in grandeur to those of
his mighty predecessors. Once more than 172 feet high and 258 feet square,
with a core of five steps and limestone casing stones, Pepi II's burial place is now
a large pile of rubble, emblematic of the collapse of the Old Kingdom. The ceilings
of the corridor and the inner chamber originally were decorated with stars.

called himself "the grand chieftain." His tomb inscriptions speak of decisive action to stave off hunger—the cultivation of sandbanks in the middle of the river and the closing of provincial boundaries to prevent aimless wandering. Rumors of cannibalism swirl around this desperate period. Ankhtifi seems to have achieved some success. He boasted: "My equal has not and will not come into being."

Another district headman, Khety of Asyut, grew up at the royal court and learned swimming with the pharaoh's children in the carefree days of his youth. As soon as he became a nomarch far upstream of Thebes, his troubles multiplied. Low floods brought hunger in their train. Thousands of acres of farmland received no floodwater at all. His officials sedulously hoarded grain. Khety's tomb tells the story: "I nourished my town…as giver of water…. I made a dam…when Upper Egypt was a desert…. I was rich in grain when the land was as a sandbank."

The nomarchs knew their districts well and had strong roots in the countryside. They had learned the hard way that only decisive action could alleviate hunger. They closed provincial boundaries, rationed grain, maintained tight control over their domains, tried to prevent panic, and kept an eye on their neighbors up- and downstream. Each nomarch paid nominal homage to the distant pharaoh, but they were the real rulers of Egypt because they could feed the hungry and stimulate agriculture.

Memories of the great drought endured for generations, long after Egypt once again became a powerful state. An entire literary genre was built on the evils of chaos. The writings of the sage Ipuwer graphically picture an Egypt gripped by repeated famines where "the plunderer is everywhere and the servant takes what he finds."

Upper Egypt became a dry wasteland as sand blew onto the floodplain from the encroaching desert. Neither fruit nor herbage could be found any longer. Desperate villagers attacked and looted the state granaries. "The Storehouse is bare, / Its keeper stretched on the ground…. The grain of Egypt is 'I-go-get-it.'" In a memorable passage, Ipuwer blamed the procession of ineffectual pharaohs at Memphis: "Authority, Knowledge, and Truth are with you—turmoil is what you let happen in the land, and the noise of strife." Egyptian kingship depended on the belief that the pharaoh was the son of Re, the sun god, protected by Horus, the celestial falcon deity. Pharaohs were flood-makers. So when the floods failed to materialize, the king was seen to have feet of clay. The myth of royal infallibility collapsed with the drought, and the Old Kingdom withered like a once ripe grape on the vine.

Inyotef, an 11th dynasty official, embraces his son Amenemhet, while his mother clasps him with both hands. At right, Amenemhet's wife Hapy stands by a stone offering table piled with food. The inscription reads: "Honored by Osiris, who gives an invocation offering of bread and beer, meat and fowl for the honored Amenemhet."

THE MIDDLE KINGDOM

Once limestone-cased, the mud-brick core of Middle
Kingdom Pharaoh Amenemhet III's pyramid still looms
above the desert at Hawara. The Middle Kingdom saw
Egypt rise once again to great power and prosperity.
The Theban Pharaoh Mentuhotep reunified the Two Lands
into a highly centralized state. He and his successors
thought of themselves as shepherds of the people as
much as divine kings, each ruler maintaining close trading
relations with Nubia and also with eastern Mediterranean
lands. The Middle Kingdom also saw the democratization
of eternity: Anyone could ensure themselves eternal life—
if they could afford the rituals. After Amenemhet III's
death about 1770 B.C., Middle Kingdom Egypt went into
decline, as thousands of Asians settled in the delta.
Sometime after 1630 B.C., Sheshi, a warlord from Asia,
seized the royal capital at Memphis. Egypt became two
lands once again.

First Intermediate Period

Dynasties 9 & 10
Meryibre
Khety
Merikare
Ity

Dynasty 11
Mentuhotep I
Inyotef I
Inyotef II
Inyotef III

Middle Kingdom

Dynasty 11
Mentuhotep II
(Nebhepetre)
Mentuhotep III
Mentuhotep IV

Dynasty 12
Amenemhet I
Senusret I
Amenemhet II
Senusret II
Senusret III
Amenemhet III
Amenemhet IV
Queen Sobek-nefru

Dynasty 13
Wegaf
Amenemhet V
Harnedjheriotef
Amenyqemau
Sebekhotep I
Hor
Amenemhet VII
Sebekhotep II
Khendjer
Sebekhotep III
Neferhotep I
Sebekhotep IV
Sebekhotep V
Aye
Mentuemzaf
Dedumose II
Neferhotep III

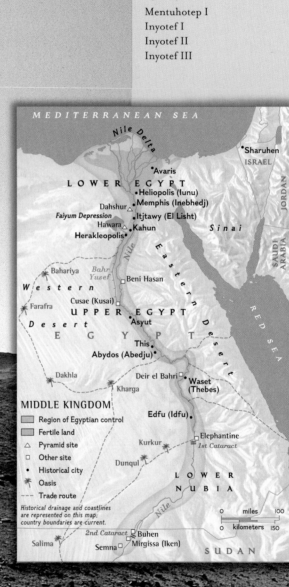

MEDITERRANEAN SEA

Nile Delta

Sharuhen
ISRAEL

Avaris

LOWER EGYPT
Heliopolis (Iunu)
Memphis (Inebhedj)
Dahshur
Faiyum Depression
Itjtawy (El Lisht)
Hawara
Kahun
Herakleopolis
Sinai

JORDAN

SAUDI ARABIA

Bahariya
Bahr Yusef
Beni Hasan

Western
Farafra
Cusae (Kusai)
UPPER EGYPT
Asyut
Desert
EGYPT
This
Abydos (Abedju)

RED SEA

Eastern Desert

Dakhla
Kharga
Deir el Bahri
Waset (Thebes)

MIDDLE KINGDOM
■ Region of Egyptian control
■ Fertile land
△ Pyramid site
□ Other site
● Historical city
✳ Oasis
--- Trade route

Historical drainage and coastlines
are represented on this map;
country boundaries are current.

Edfu (Idfu)

Elephantine
1st Cataract

Kurkur

Dunqul

LOWER NUBIA

Nile

0   miles   100
0   kilometers   150

Salima
2nd Cataract
Semna
Buhen
Mirgissa (Iken)

SUDAN

Second Intermediate	New Kingdom	Third Intermediate Period	Late Period	Greco-Roman Age
ca 1630-1520 B.C.	ca 1539-1070 B.C.	ca 1075-715 B.C.	ca 715-332 B.C.	332 B.C.-A.D. 395

Dynasty 14

Nehesy

Dynasties 15 & 16 (HYKSOS)

Sheshi
Khyan
Apepi
Khamudi

Dynasty 17

Inyotef V
Sebekemzaf I
Nebireyeraw
Sebekamzaf II
Ta'o I
Ta'o II
Kamose

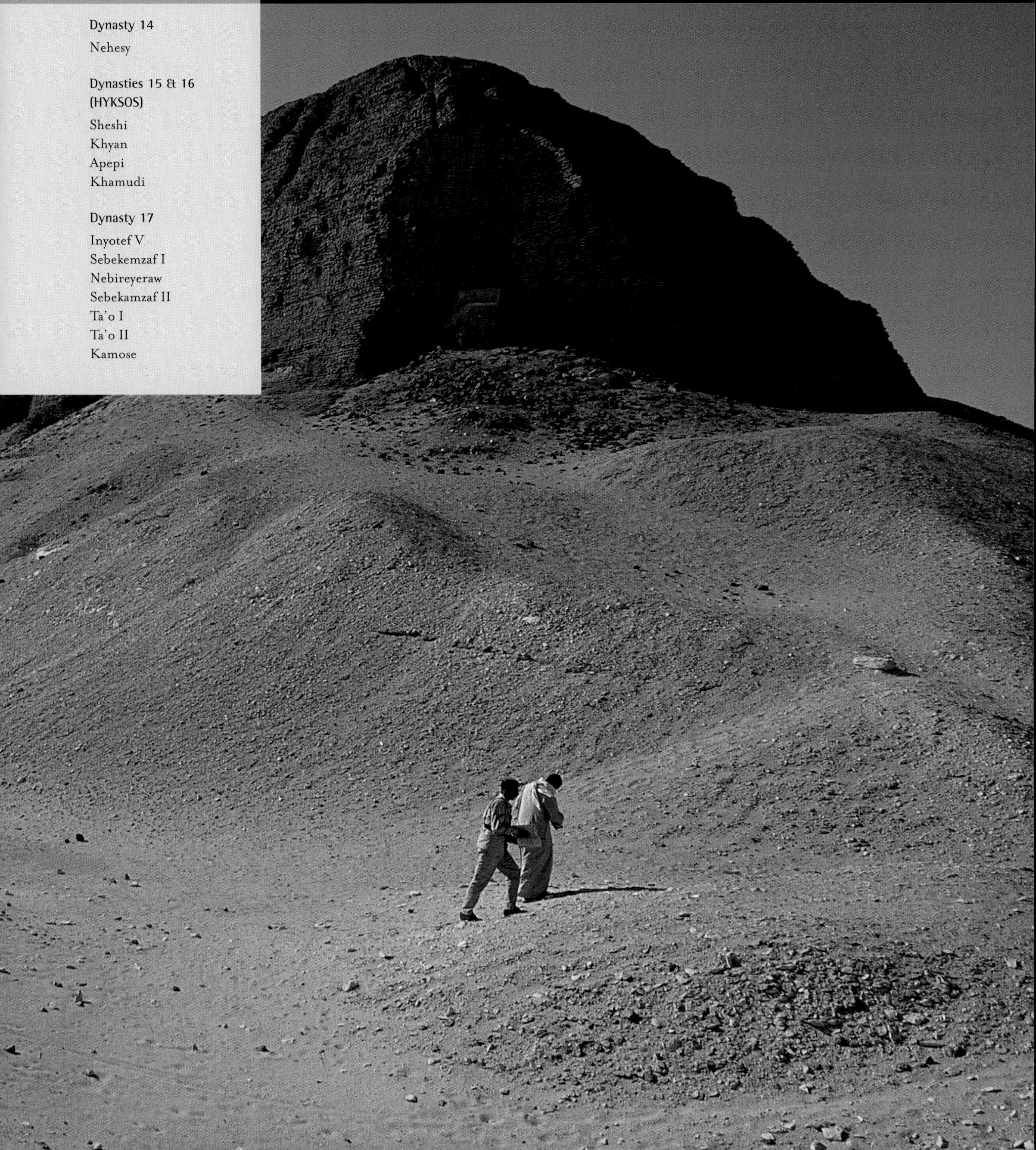

"I offered for 13 rulers without a mishap ever befalling me. I was not robbed, I was not spat in the eyes, owing to the worth of my speech, the competence of my counsel, and the bending of my arm. I did what the great ones liked. ... I have bowed brow and feather." The butler Merer of Edfu, a town in Upper Egypt, lived through the turbulence and power struggles that followed the demise of Pepi II. He was the consummate official, discreet, bending easily with the political winds. Merer did not serve 13 nomarchs; rather, he merely made the appropriate offerings to dead superiors as well as living ones—and boasted of his service on his mortuary stela.

A lifelike portrait mask (above) celebrates the individualism of Middle Kingdom art. A wooden model found in the chancellor Meketre's tomb (ca 2100 B.C.) shows servants parading Meketre's cattle past a shady arbor where the family sits to view the procession.

Pharaoh Nebhepetre Mentuhotep II of the 11th dynasty wears the Red Crown
of Lower Egypt and the tight-fitting white Heb-sed costume used for his jubilee
celebration. During his long 50-year reign this pharaoh reunited Egypt. His crossed
arms and black face symbolically indicate the pharaoh's connection with Osiris,
ruler of the underworld and the god of death and rebirth.

One of Merer's contemporaries, the treasurer Iti of the town of Imyotru, proclaimed himself a "great pillar in the Theban nome, a man of standing in the Southland." Such "men of standing" were the backbone of an Upper Egypt fractured by the petty rivalries of ambitious nomarchs. Their passion for order and deep sense of responsibility for the towns and villages under their jurisdictions pulled a now divided country through the worst crisis in a thousand years. Nomarch might fight nomarch, but the officials behind them maintained at least a semblance of administrative control. Ancient loyalties and village ties always ran deep in Egypt, and the ultimate power of Merer, Iti, and their ilk lay as much among village headmen as in their lords' palaces.

The fighting and rivalries in Upper Egypt intensified as the great drought weakened and normal inundations returned. Each victorious nomarch had his eye on a larger prize—the kingship itself. By 2125 B.C., the rulers of Herakleopolis near modern Beni Suef had won control of the middle reaches of Egypt. They soon quarreled with the ambitious ruling family of Thebes, the Greek name for the city of Waset, who presided over a separate kingdom upstream. Constant border clashes erupted as Thebes tried to subdue the territory of its northern rival. After 2080 B.C., three rich Theban rulers, all named Inyotef, tried repeatedly to overthrow Herakleopolis. The treasurer Tjetji served Inyotef II and III, presided over a treasury bursting with "everything that gladdens the heart, being the best of every good thing brought...as tribute from this entire land."

The Inyotefs were now openly proclaiming themselves sons of Re and kings of Upper and Lower Egypt. Each pushed the Theban boundary farther downstream beyond Abydos and This. By the time of Inyotef III's death in about 1975 B.C., the Theban domain extended from the First Cataract almost to Asyut on the middle Nile.

Nebhepetre Mentuhotep II resumed where his predecessor left off. His birth name meant "Montu is content," Montu being the god of war. Both expert politician and warrior, he soon assumed new Horus names: "He who gives heart to the Two Lands" and "Lord of the White Crown [Upper Egypt]." Bitter fighting marked the first 14 years of Mentuhotep's reign, both on his northern frontier and against his immediate rivals. Shrewdly, he gained control of lucrative trade routes and campaigned in Nubia, recruiting hard-fighting Nubian mercenaries, who fought alongside Egyptians in his army. A fine wooden model from the tomb of an official named Mesehti at Asyut depicts two 40-man detachments of Egyptian spearmen and Nubian archers marching in formation. The decisive moment came when This and the holy town of Abydos rose in revolt. Mentuhotep descended in wrath and put down the rebellion after a series of bloody battles. Victory followed victory until he controlled Memphis and Lower Egypt and assumed yet another Horus name, "Uniter of the Two Lands." By 1971 B.C. Mentuhotep was master of all Egypt, so he turned his attention to consolidating his frontiers in Nubia and the Sinai.

Mentuhotep's campaigns came at a high price in human lives. In 1911 American Egyptologist Herbert Winlock excavated the pharaoh's mortuary temple on the west bank of the Nile near Thebes and unearthed the sepulchre of 60 soldiers killed in battle. The bodies were stacked like logs in the tomb, each wrapped in linen shrouds. All the soldiers were in the prime of life with their hair cut off at the nape of the neck. Every one of them had met a violent end from arrows or from blows to the head. Winlock studied the wounds carefully and reconstructed a vicious battle before a fortress where stones and ebony-tipped arrows rained down on the attackers. Contemporary pictures of sieges show defenders lining fortified battlements as the attackers approach with scaling ladders or try to undermine the defenses with only flimsy shields protecting them from the shower of deadly missiles. This particular attack had failed. The soldiers withdrew under fire, taking fatal wounds in the back as they retreated. The defenders now sallied forth and killed the wounded with clubs—several of the dead infantrymen died from savage blows to the left side of their heads, just like coup de grace blows given by Egyptian warriors to crippled enemies in reliefs of the period. The ever present ravens and vultures hovered overhead looking for a meal. The carrion birds pecked at the slain until a successful counterattack captured the fort. The pharaoh ordered the mangled corpses buried honorably in a special tomb at his mortuary temple.

Egypt recovered quickly from the divisive civil war. Prosperity returned to the land even though there were political tensions under the surface. Mentuhotep rewarded his highest officials with fine estates, where they lived in style. In 1920 Winlock examined the much looted tomb of the king's chancellor Meketre and recovered an astounding portrait of life on a great estate. While making a plan of the rubble-filled tomb, chips and dust kept dropping through a crack at the base of a wall. Winlock shone a flashlight into the gap and onto "a little world of four thousand years ago, a busy going and coming...in uncanny silence, as though the distance back...was too great for even an echo to reach my ears."

Meketre had followed the custom of his day and commissioned wooden models of everyday activities to ensure their continuation in the next life. Twenty-five detailed models chronicle daily life on the chancellor's estate. His porticoed house with flat roof and brightly painted columns looks out over a tree-shaded garden pool. A servant girl wears a short white sheath adorned with a bead net. She carries two offering jars in a box on her head and a live duck clasped in her left hand. In another scene Meketre and his family sit under a shaded arbor as workers parade spotted cattle before him. The tableau of painted figures bore the fingerprints of those who had stored them in the tomb. Also found: a model carpentry shop complete with artisans at work and a chest of spare tools; bakers' and butchers' shops; the lord's boat flotilla; even the kitchen tender.

Pharaoh Mentuhotep had his tomb and mortuary temple placed in an amphitheater of cliffs at Deir el-Bahri on the west bank opposite Thebes. There his architects erected a giant terrace tomb reached by a sloping causeway. A walkway led to the central edifice, a colonnaded building capped with either a cornice or, some people believe, a pyramid. A cloistered court surrounded the entrance to the king's subterranean tomb. A 492-foot-long tunnel, descending through solid rock, continued to a magnificent burial chamber 147 feet below the court. The king's alabaster shrine filled the chamber, surrounded by chips of expensive black diorite. A stone hypostyle hall with 80 octagonal columns, the first ever constructed in Egypt, led from the court to a niche in the rock where a statue of Mentuhotep once stood, so sited to give the impression that the pharaoh was emerging from the mountain. (A hypostyle hall was a chamber with many columns that symbolized the reeds of the primordial marsh.) The el-Qurn peak towers high above the royal burial place like a symbolic pyramid.

KINGSHIP IS AGAIN WHAT IT WAS IN THE PAST

During the short reign of Mentuhotep III (ca 1948-1938 B.C.), the vizier and governor of the south, Amenemhet, went on an expedition to the quarries of the Wadi Hammamat in the Eastern Desert in search of a fine block of smooth hard rock for the lid of his master's sarcophagus. With him traveled an army of 10,000 men to disperse hostile nomads on the way. An inscription on the south side of the wadi records how a pregnant gazelle led the way to a suitable boulder and dropped her young on the rock. She was promptly sacrificed on it, and a miraculous shower of rain fell on the dry gully. Amenemhet's men used bronze chisels to dislodge the block, then levered it onto a sledge for the long journey to the Nile. The stone may never have honored the king. About 1938 B.C., having returned to Egypt with his army at his back, the vizier Amenemhet promptly overthrew Mentuhotep and declared himself pharaoh.

TOMB PAINTINGS AND RELIEFS

A wife of Pharaoh Nebhepetre Mentuhotep of the 11th dynasty, 22-year-old Queen Ashait was buried near the king in a mortuary complex at Deir el-Bahri on the west bank of the Nile at Thebes. Ashait lay in a magnificent sculptured limestone sarcophagus where she is seen receiving an offering of a duck (right) while a girl fans her from behind. Paintings like the one above decorated the interior of her tomb. Ashait's mummy survived intact, together with a wooden funerary statuette of the queen wearing a long red skirt with shoulder straps and gold bracelets. Her body exhibits none of the pathologies suffered by commoners. Ashait lived amid the luxury of the court. Her long, slender arms show no signs of muscle development from repetitive tasks. One hand is long-fingered and elegant, her nails beautifully manicured and stained red with henna. A social chasm separated Ashait and her companions from commoners, but all were susceptible to fatal infections in an era without antibiotics.

Amenemhet was a commoner by birth, his mother coming from the Elephantine region. Like many other high officials of the day he had risen from obscurity by sheer ability. He took over a kingdom seething with potential unrest. Mentuhotep had curbed many of the nomarchs' powers, but some of the provincial governors still acted like kings, even maintaining their own armies and fleets. Amenemhet promptly cruised the river with his warships and loyal regiments in a formidable show of strength, but his rule over the Two Lands was never comfortable. He was a southerner with strong loyalties to Thebes. For political reasons, however, he founded a fortified capital named Itjtawy, "Seizer of the Two Lands," downstream some 20 miles south of Memphis and remote from any existing power centers.

While keeping a watchful eye on his kingdom, Amenemhet I worried about the succession. He had already taken the name Wehem-meswet, "Repeater-of-Births," to signal that he was the start of a new kingly line. Now he established an important precedent by bringing in his son Senusret as co-regent in the 20th year of his reign. The king had already campaigned deep into Lower Nubia and established garrisons there. Senusret took over the army, consolidated gains in Nubia, and patrolled the eastern and western frontiers. He was on an expedition against the "sand-dwellers" of the Western Desert when his father was murdered by his courtiers. The young prince hurried back to the capital, suppressed the nascent coup, and assumed the throne, to reign for 45 years.

Senusret consolidated the wise policies of his father. A remarkable document, claimed to be instructions from the assassinated Amenemhet for his son, may have guided his actions. The powerful and imaginative words of the *Instruction of Amenemhet,* said to have come to Senusret in a revelation, are remarkable for their bitterness born of long experience. The dead pharaoh advises his son to trust no one:

Risen as god, hear what I tell you, / That you may rule the land, govern the shores, / Increase well-being! / Beware of subjects who are nobodies, / Of whose plotting one is not aware. / Trust not a brother, know not a friend, / Make no intimates, it is worthless.

"As my feet depart, you are in my heart," he ends. "Jubilation is in the bark of Re, kingship is again what it was in the past!" The message was clear: Pharaohs were no longer infallible and could not assume that divine prestige alone would keep them in power.

The young king took his father's words to heart and maintained a firm hand on the reins of government. In the third year of his reign he dedicated a rebuilt temple to Re-Atum at Heliopolis, the center of the sun cult, and inscribed an account of his deed on

FOLLOWING PAGES: In the tomb of the 11th dynasty official Mesehti, at Asyut, fine wooden models portray military detachments, each 40-strong, marching in formation. Here a regiment of Nubian bowmen wear short linen kilts and have standardized hairdos. For centuries Nubians served bravely as highly regarded mercenaries in the pharaohs' armies.

a stela, copied centuries later by a New Kingdom scribe. Apparently the pharaoh attended the foundation ceremony in person: "The king appeared in the double crown; a sitting took place in the audience hall, a consultation with his followers, the companions of the palace.... Command was uttered for them to hear; counsel was given for them to learn." The following day Senusret appeared "in the plumed crown, with all the people following him. The chief lector-priest and scribe of the divine books stretched the cord. The rope was released, laid in the ground, made to be this temple. His majesty.... turned round before the people. Joined together were Upper and Lower Egypt."

Senusret traveled constantly to maintain a high profile. His firm hand was everywhere, supervising major festivals, visiting his governors, mounting mining expeditions into the desert. He consolidated earlier gains in Nubia with a network of fortified settlements and trading stations as far upstream as the Second Cataract.

The prestige of the pharaohs as gods had declined, but they were constantly praised as forceful administrators. They now proclaimed that the sun god Re had charged them to establish and enforce ma'at on earth. The lessons of the great drought were not forgotten. Middle Kingdom pharaohs saw themselves as shepherds of the people as much as omnipotent kings, more concerned with the common welfare than their predecessors. They were also believers in centralized control and imposed a firm bureaucracy on every aspect of Egyptian life.

Senusret seems to have been a wise and generous monarch if the oft-told *Story of Sinuhe* is any guide. Generations of Egyptian children learned the tale in school. Sinuhe is a young attendant in the royal palace. He flees in terror at the plotting against the king and crosses the Sinai, making his way by night across the fortified frontier known as "Walls of the Ruler." After taking refuge with a band of nomads, he travels on to Byblos. In Syria he is well received by the Palestinian Prince of Retenu, who marries him to his eldest daughter. Sinuhe becomes a successful landowner and warrior, raises a family, and grows old, "wealthy in goods, rich in herds." But he hankers to return to the land of his birth. Senusret hears of his wish and sends messages of welcome: "Come back to Egypt! See the residence in which you lived! Kiss the ground at the great portals, mingle with the courtiers!" He granted Sinuhe the privilege of a fine tomb. "You shall not die abroad! Not shall Asiatics inter you! You shall not be wrapped in the skin of a ram to serve as your coffin. Too long a roaming of the earth! Think of your corpse, come back!" Sinuhe returns home in triumph, is welcomed by the pharaoh, and lives happily ever after. Pure fiction, of course, but the story resonates with authenticity. *(Continued on page 140)*

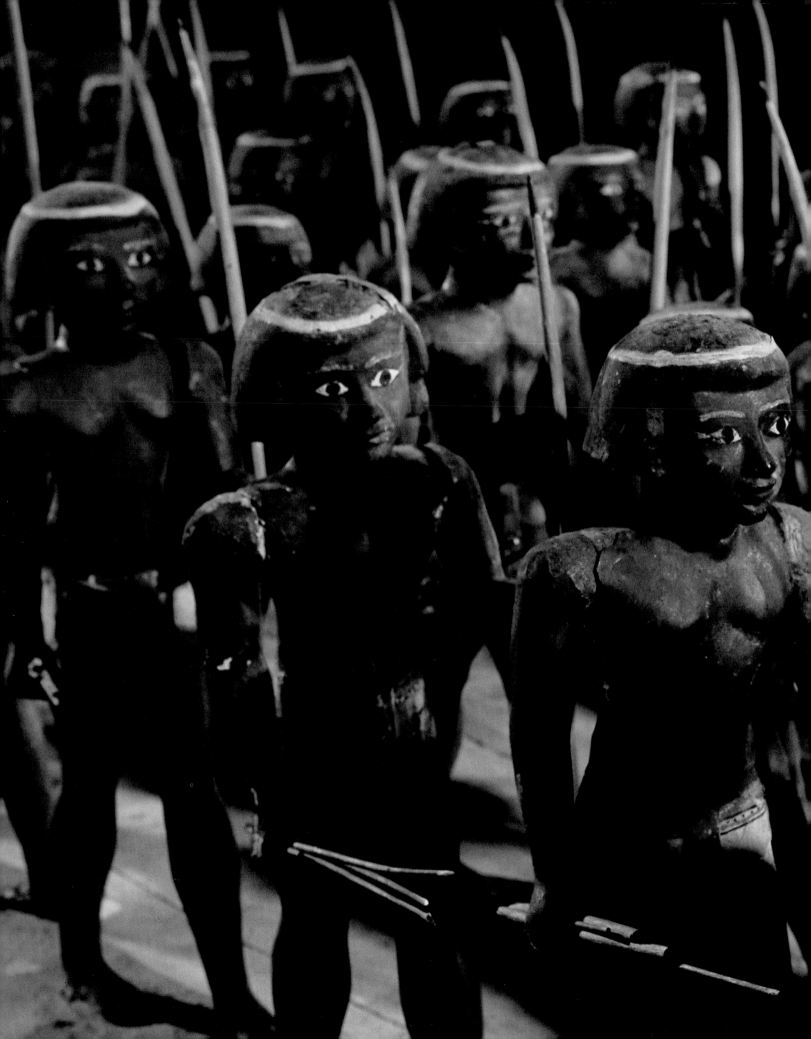

Another well known Middle Kingdom document, *The Prophecy of Neferti,* recounts in a historical romance genre how the prophet Neferti, "a great lector-priest of Bastet...a citizen with valiant arm, a scribe excellent with his fingers," is summoned to the 4th dynasty court of King Snefru to entertain with "choice phrases." Neferti bewailed the appalling state of the country where "The land is quite perished, no remnant is left....Dry is the river of Egypt, one crosses the water on foot." But there was hope:

> *Then a king will come from the South, / Ameny [Amenemhet], the justified, by name..../*
> *He will take the White Crown, / He will wear the Red Crown. / He will join the Two Mighty Ones.*

Egypt would be reunited, her frontiers secured against thieving Asiatics by the "Wall of the Ruler." Then "Order will return to its seat, While Chaos is driven away."

Neferti's panegyric was royal propaganda, recited by schoolchildren for centuries, justifying the deeds of remote, but human, monarchs who protected their people against the forces of chaos that always lingered beyond the frontiers. Their portraits brood over their temples and the kingdom, showing competent men who took their responsibilities as shepherds of the people very seriously. At the same time the wealth and splendor of the court with its brilliant artisans and panoply of high officials separated the ruler from the ruled by a deep chasm that persisted through life into death.

At least two years before his death Senusret I took his son Amenemhet II as co-regent, who became pharaoh in about 1876 B.C. Amenemhet II was a consolidator, who spent much of his 34-year reign concerned about agricultural production and food supplies. He recognized the potential of the Faiyum depression west of the Nile with its abundant fish, fowl, wildlife, and fertile soils. A canal, now known as Bahr Yusef, linked the Nile and the Faiyum. He and his successors caused it to be deepened and widened, bringing thousands of acres of dry land under intensive irrigation for the first time.

SENUSRET IS SATISFIED

Senusret and his successors never forgot the lessons of the great drought. They placed much importance on the orderliness of government, promoted able officials, many of them commoners, and kept the reins of power firmly in hand. They invested heavily in agriculture, storage facilities, and other public works, as well as their own sepulchres. Their mantra was efficient administration and control, which resulted not only in a bureaucratic central government but also one whose tentacles reached deep into the countryside and into the remotest communities.

Toward the end of the 19th century the great Egyptologist Flinders Petrie excavated the pyramid of Senusret II, who died about 1837 B.C. Known mainly for his agricultural works in the Faiyum, Senusret founded a town named Hetep-Senusret ("Senusret is satisfied"), now known as Kahun, near the entrance to the Faiyum depression. Here lived the workers who labored on his pyramid and mortuary temple as well as the priests and lay people who supervised the king's mortuary cults. Kahun continued to flourish into the 13th dynasty (ca 1755-1630 B.C.), long after the king's death.

Kahun was a square, walled town of more than 3,000 people with an internal street grid. The larger houses had blank brick walls, broken only by the door spaces at front and back. They consisted not only of residential quarters but also of storage areas such as granaries, a kitchen, a cattle shed, and other domestic rooms. Their granaries were capable of holding large stocks—altogether having the capacity to store enough grain for 5,000 people on full rations. Most dwellings were much smaller and built in rows, often back-to-back. This reflects a highly organized society with strict demarcations of social rank and a town that was run as a carefully administered community where most of the inhabitants lived off rations issued by those who dwelt in the larger residences. Kahun also had its own temple dedicated to Sepdu, Lord of the East.

What kind of people lived in Kahun? The town papyrus archives enable us to identify a mayor as well as an "office of the vizier," where an official would go to conduct legal proceedings and administer oaths. There was a administrative office that supervised a subdivision called "the area of the northern district," another office for a "reporter" (a senior official who conducted trials), and a prison. One census document inventories the household of a priest named Khakaura-Snefru. He lived in a large residence with his wife, son, and daughter. This priest also controlled the services of female "serfs," 13 of them allocated to his position as priest, others given to him by another official, and 13 whom he inherited from the sister of his father. Khakaura-Snefru presided over a relatively modest establishment. Another official of the day at Thebes had 95 serfs, more than half of them Asiatics, mostly women. The men were listed as domestic servants or field laborers, cooks, tutors, even sandalmakers. Many of the women were clothmakers, one a hairdresser, another a gardener.

The Kahun papyri also identify more specialized occupations: soldiers and scribes, doorkeepers, even foreign singers and male and female dancers. Zealous scribes inventoried every household, like those of two soldiers, Hori and his son Snefru, which changed

The White Crown of Upper Egypt adorns the head of Pharaoh Senusret I
(ca 1918-1875 B.C.). This exquisite wooden statue of the king carrying a long
crook comes from the tomb of a loyal subject, the high priest Imhotep of Iunu,
buried on the east side of his pharaoh's pyramid.

constantly over the years: some people were born and others died, some were inherited from relatives, and others were relatives who came to live with them. At times as many as nine people belonged to Hori's household.

The officials who laid out Kahun, admittedly a "government town," saw society as having only two levels: that of top officials with large households and the rest. Reality was more complex. Dozens of residential units were dependent on larger ones, and the population of Kahun's households constantly ebbed and flowed as residents moved from town to their home communities in the countryside. After the Middle Kingdom the pharaohs gave up planned communities other than those for small groups of workers. Society was simply too complex.

A town like Kahun—designed to service royal mortuary cults—lies close to Abydos but outside the ancient city. The bureaucracy also carefully supervised small workers' settlements, such as the isolated quarrymen's town at Qasr el-Sagha on the northwestern edge of the Faiyum depression. The brick-built community lies close to the former shoreline of the Faiyum lake at the end of a paved road that led to basalt quarries in the surrounding hills. The officials who erected the town aligned the walls to the cardinal points of the compass with as much care as a major temple or town in the Nile Valley.

"I HAVE MADE MY BOUNDARY FARTHER SOUTH"

Thus boasted Pharaoh Senusret III in about 1820 B.C., after fortifying the Nubian frontier at the Second Cataract in the 16th year of his reign. The fortresses he built served as bases for military expeditions to police trade routes between the Nubian kingdom of Kerma (the capital or base for the Kushites) farther upstream and Lower Nubia.

I have made my boundary farther south than my fathers, / I have added to what was bequeathed to me. / I am a king who speaks and acts, / What my heart plans is done by my arm. / "One who attacks to conquer, who is swift to succeed, / In whose heart a plan does not slumber."

The Egyptian priest Manetho, who compiled a list of dynasties, tells us Senusret was a mighty warrior and a man of great height: 4 cubits, 3 palms, 2 fingers tall: more than 6 feet 6 inches. He epitomized the competent pharaohs of the Middle Kingdom, who were, above all, expert administrators, not the remote despots and mighty monarchs of earlier times. His seated granite statue bears the tired, world-weary features of a ruler who took his duties to the kingdom and the gods very seriously. Senusret III's portrait shows him not as a god, but as a living king, with responsibility for security and the earthly needs of his people. His predecessors had wrestled constantly with the problem of the powerful hereditary nomarchs of Upper Egypt, who had flouted the central government during the drought and still had political ambitions. Years of flattery, distribution of honors and privileges, and a quiet campaign to cajole many such men into entering the king's service had added to the authority of the central government. Senusret III now felt secure enough to abolish the post of nomarch. He divided the country into two departments, or *waret,* one controlling the north from the delta to Asyut, the "Head of the South," the other from Asyut south to Aswan and Lower Nubia. A vizier, responsible directly to the king, presided over each waret with his own staff.

Few pharaohs could have succeeded with this bold reorganization, which must have had the effect of dramatically reducing the threat of political fragmentation for the first time in generations. Not that anyone would lightly challenge a warrior of Senusret's caliber. His physical stature alone was enough to intimidate even the most ambitious nomarch.

Once the internal security of the country was assured and government in the hands of his own loyalists, Senusret turned his attention to foreign policy, especially to control of the lucrative Nubian trade. During the Old Kingdom, Egypt had dominated the sparsely inhabited reaches of Lower Nubia above the First Cataract and raided the more populated areas farther upstream. Now the Middle Kingdom pharaohs pressed southward in their ambition to control the increasingly lucrative ivory and gold trade.

The Nubians were formidable enemies. Many of their commanders and soldiers had long served bravely in the Egyptian army and had taken the measure of their enemy. A confrontation was inevitable, especially when the aggressive Nubian chiefs of Kerma near the Third Cataract extended their influence over Lower Nubia, which the Egyptians considered their own. In about 1930 B.C., Amenemhet I had boasted: "I subdued lions, I captured crocodiles, I suppressed the people of Wawat [Lower Nubia]." In reality his expedition may have killed numerous villagers, but he obtained no permanent military advantage. His son Senusret I built some forts between the First to Second Cataracts to establish a stronger Egyptian presence in the region.

Senusret III (ca 1836-1818 B.C.) garrisoned Lower Nubia with a row of fortresses that stretched from the First Cataract to Semna, 250 miles upstream. "I have made my boundary farther south than my fathers," he boasted on a pair of boundary stelae that he erected at Semna, the southernmost of his forts, at the end of the strategic Second

FOLLOWING PAGES: Multiple life-size statues in limestone of King Senusret I gaze into space from their seats on blocklike thrones. Found outside Senusret I's mortuary temple at Lisht in 1894, their purpose remains unknown. Did they grace the temple's interior, or were they, perhaps, abandoned before being used?

Cataract region. He described the Nubians as cowards, "not people he [Senusret] respects, they are wretches, craven-hearted." The inscriptions tell of the men he killed and of the women and children he enslaved, the cattle he slaughtered, the crops he burned. To encourage his successors, he set up a statue of himself "at this border which my majesty has made so that you maintain it and so that you fight for it."

The figures on the stela glowered downstream at a row of imposing fortresses that stretched as far as Elephantine at the very gates of Egypt itself. The most impressive fortress of all was Buhen, at a critical strategic point at the foot of the Second Cataract, a vast mud-brick construction that had much of the sophistication and impregnability of a European medieval castle. The fort had originated as an Old Kingdom mining station built on a gently shelving plateau adjacent to the Nile. A dense Nubian population cultivated the fertile land on the opposite bank.

Military architects in the Middle Kingdom were well aware of the damage that could be done by siege engines, which had come into use perhaps during the civil wars that preceded unification. So they fortified this remote outpost accordingly and built a stone-lined passageway under the northern gate to ensure a reliable water supply in times of siege. The fortress faced the river, defined by a massive mud-brick enclosure wall up to 28 feet tall and 13 feet thick with external towers.

A single gateway on the desert side was protected by two parallel walls with their own towers and a drawbridge so that an attacker was automatically under fire from the flanks. A ditch and rampart with its own parapet protected the base of the enclosure wall, which was equipped with small towers and loopholes for archers.

Buhen was to all intents and purposes impregnable. Inside stood the garrison headquarters backed up against the main wall in the northwest corner, a temple, and barrack buildings erected around a grid of streets.

TRADE BY RIVER, LAND, AND SEA

At the Second Cataract itself Senusret III built a group of forts to protect the narrow Semna Gorge where the Nile flows through a rocky barrier. His architects cleverly tailored the fortifications to the rocky outcrops by the river, erecting smaller ones heavily defended against ever sophisticated siege machinery. The entire Second Cataract complex was a state-of-the-art defensive work complete with outlying lookout towers. Senusret's commanders were not content merely to remain behind

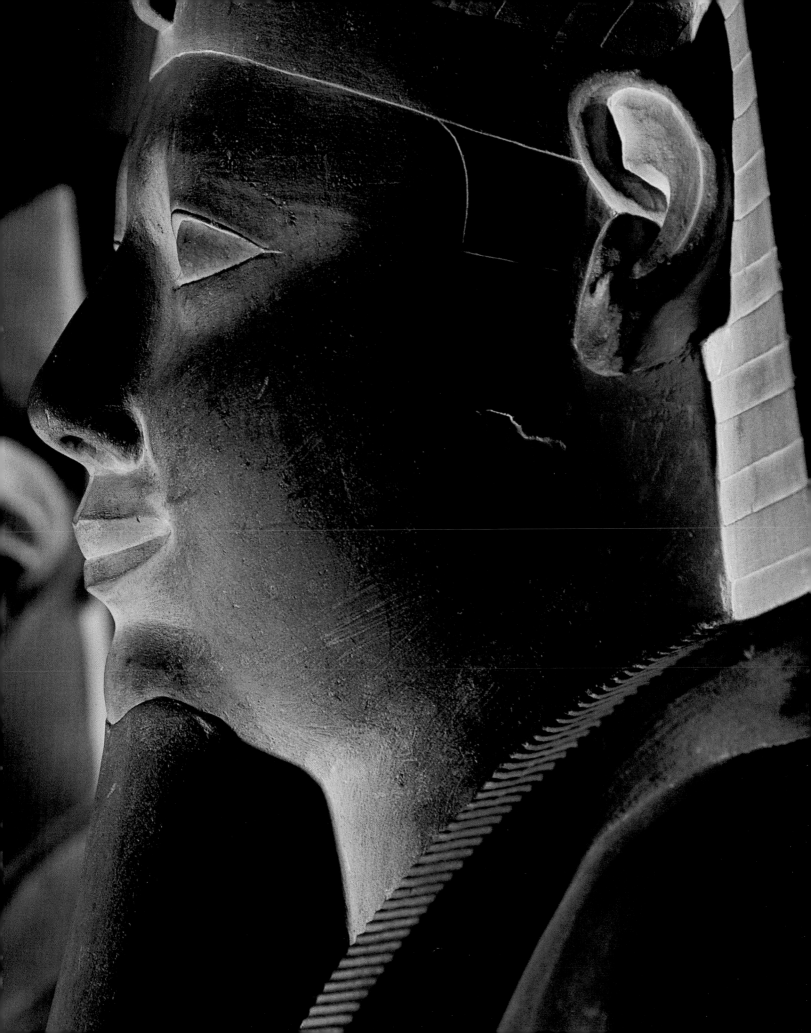

In a masterpiece of Middle Kingdom craftsmanship, a blue faience hippopotamus found at Thebes stands resolutely on dry land. Holding court in great splendor at a time of unprecedented prosperity built on foreign trade, Middle Kingdom pharaohs patronized architects and artists to brilliant effect. Jewelers created ornaments in gold and semiprecious stones, and faience manufacture reached new heights.

fortified walls. They maintained active surveillance over the surrounding desert with constant patrols. Reports written during the reign of Senusret III's son Amenemhet III reveal how the Egyptians used Nubian Medjay, or desert nomads, on these excursions and probably paid them with grain. The terse dispatches report sightings of caravans. "We have found a track of 32 men and 3 donkeys," states one such report. The purpose of the entire operation was to maintain and control trade and diplomatic activities with the increasingly powerful and wealthy Nubian kingdom of Kerma, or Kush, upstream.

All Nile trade funneled through the fort of Mirgissa (Iken) at the upstream end of the Second Cataract and about 12 miles south of the frontier at Semna. Here the authorities maintained large granaries and a mud-lubricated slipway to help traders drag their boats past the rapids. Another fortress, Askut, located on an island upstream of Semna, housed an enormous granary, perhaps an emergency supply or rear depot for feeding the surrounding forts and military expeditions beyond the frontier.

Senusret's entire Nubian operation was a carefully regulated military strategy designed to secure trade routes and protect the southern frontier. The forts themselves served both as garrisons and as spots on a chain of military supply that extended deep into Nubia. Senusret never conquered Kerma to make it a colony, but he left such a powerful impression in Nubia that he was later worshiped there as a local deity.

The Nubian investment was critical to Egypt, which depended heavily on gold and other minerals to support its economy. Gold was a divine substance, the flesh of the gods. The sun god Re was sometimes called "mountain of gold," while his daughter Hathor was known as "the golden one." The Egyptians gilded the tips of obelisks and pyramids to emphasize their links to the sun, while the golden death masks of pharaohs symbolized their transformation into gods at death. The government maintained enormous stocks of gold, much of which ultimately vanished underground into royal sepulchres and those of high officials. The military supervised most gold mining, often carried out by prisoners of war and foreign workers. A team of officials oversaw the work—an expedition commander and his deputies, also the usual scribes, as well as cooks, animal drivers, and expert miners. Silver, a sacred metal, was virtually unobtainable in Egypt.

Egypt had been in irregular touch with Asia for many centuries, with the cedar trade in particular being a cherished royal monopoly for a long period. The 12th and 13th dynasty pharaohs (ca 1938-1630 B.C.) strengthened these ties as demand for both essentials and luxuries intensified. Egyptian objects of this period have come from ancient cities in the Levant, among them Byblos and Megiddo. Byblos had particularly close ties to Egypt; her

rulers adopted Egyptian royal titulary and used hieroglyphs. They even adopted forms of Egyptian royal regalia. The pharaohs mined copper and turquoise aggressively in the Sinai Desert. Donkey caravans regularly crossed the desert overland with goods from Asia.

Most Asian imports came by sea, carried along coastal shipping routes: to the Nile Delta from the eastern Mediterranean coast, from the great ports of Ugarit and elsewhere, which were crossroads of the eastern Mediterranean world. Here traders from many lands obtained shipments of cedar wood, copper from Cyprus, tin from Anatolia (now Turkey), and luxuries and basic commodities from farther to the east—from the Euphrates Valley and Mesopotamia. Merchant ships from the Levant coasted westward along what is now the Turkish shore to Rhodes, Crete, and the distant Aegean Islands.

Egyptian artifacts of the 12th and 13th dynasties found in Cretan palaces document regular ties with the seafaring Minoan civilization. Crete, known to the Egyptians as Keftiu, yielded olive oil, timber, and wool, for which she received linen and papyrus, beads, pendants, and fine scarabs. Stone vessels and faience vases of characteristic Egyptian form found their way to Crete in considerable numbers, some of them inscribed with royal names, as if they were formal gifts. In the 14th century A.D. heavily laden cargo ships— like the celebrated Uluburun vessel shipwrecked off the Turkish coast in a

PATRONS OF THE GODS

Every Middle Kingdom pharaoh lavished wealth on
the gods, and King Senusret I (ca 1918-1875 B.C.) was
no exception. His reconstructed White Chapel (right),
at Karnak, was destroyed when later royal builders
of the 18th dynasty reused blocks from it as filling
for a pylon of the Temple of Amun. This architectural
masterpiece, one of the first Middle Kingdom temples,
lavishly displays inscriptions and representational art.
The carved walls depict Senusret being embraced by
Amun, Atum, Horus, and Ptah, each god placed at
a cardinal point of the Earth. The reliefs include one
of Senusret being led by Horus into the presence
of Amun-Min, the god of fertility (above). Senusret
was an energetic pharaoh who ruled at a time of great
change in the eastern Mediterranean. He garrisoned
Nubia, exploited mines in Asia, and built numerous
temples. He also tightened the administration of the
state during an era that later Egyptians considered
a high point of their civilization.

Middle Kingdom Egyptians spent large sums in their quest for an eternity available to all who could pay the price. Only the wealthy few could afford the expensive, full mummification process. Skilled artisans lavished care on masks, such as this, that bore realistic likenesses of the deceased.

sudden squall—probably sailed direct from Crete to the Nile. There is no reason why they should not have done so in earlier centuries.

THE AFTERLIFE AND ITS DEMOCRATIZATION

The priest Ikhernofret organized the mysteries of Osiris for his master King Senusret III. "I decked the breast of the lord of Abydos with lapis lazuli and turquoise, fine gold, and all costly stones which are the ornaments of a god's body. I clothed the god with his regalia in my rank of master of secrets. . . ." A grand procession of three barks bore the god's statue from his temple to his tomb, "following the god in his steps. I made the god's boat sail, Thoth steering the sailing." One can imagine the bustling scene: Officials scurrying to and fro, busy with last-minute preparations, Ikhernofret in his gleaming priestly regalia watching calmly under an awning, the huge white sail of the gilded barge jamming while being hoisted. The sacred bark moves into the main channel of the river, and the people crowding the banks cheer. Such brilliantly adorned boats moved slowly along the riverbank in one of the most important religious processions of the year, a public reenactment of the god's kingship, death, and resurrection. Osiris's death and rebirth symbolized his ability to renew the Earth and restore life to the state.

Resurrection and eternity had once been the prerogative of royalty. But by the end of the Old Kingdom the democratization of resurrection had begun. Although the nomarchs who reunified Egypt appropriated the style and ritual of royal burial for themselves, they were buried not in pyramids but in humbler rock-cut tombs. Nebhepetre Mentuhotep reverted to a more grandiose funerary style. His mortuary complex with its platforms and colonnaded courts was situated near Thebes, with his high officials and nobles buried nearby.

The transfer of the capital from Thebes to Itjtawy during the 12th dynasty saw a renewal of burial downstream. Amenemhet and Senusret I were laid to rest under pyramids at Lisht, whose architecture owes much to the pyramids of later Old Kingdom pharaohs like Pepi II. The two kings lay in beautifully made sarcophagi placed in well-built burial chambers, but their pyramids were poorly constructed—founded on natural rock outcrops, then erected by filling interior walls with rubble or mud brick. Exterior casing stones stabilized the pyramids, but they were easy targets for tomb robbers and soon collapsed when pulled apart for their stone. Later Middle Kingdom pharaohs were

buried under pyramids at Kahun and Dahshur, accompanied by the mastabas of their most important officials, for the grant of a tomb in the royal necropolis was still a privilege. Nevertheless, burial close to the king now had a lesser significance, in large part because of the rise of the more democratic cult of Osiris.

Osiris was among the most ancient of Egyptian gods, revered as early as the 1st dynasty as one of the first nine gods, the so-called Ennead, one of the five children of Nut, the goddess of the sky, and Geb, the god of the earth. Osiris was Geb's eldest son, who married his sister Isis and became king of the earth. Osiris first appears as a deity in connection with the dead in the Pyramid Texts of the Old Kingdom. Wearing his royal mummy wrappings and the White Crown of Egypt, he was associated with Abydos, burial place of the earliest rulers. Old Kingdom pharaohs received the immortality bestowed by Osiris.

With the conquest of Abydos by the Thebans the Osiris cult became more democratic. Individuals who craved immortality adopted the after-death title "The Osiris." When 13th dynasty scholars identified the tomb of the early pharaoh Djer as that of Osiris, the sepulchre became a place of offering and pilgrimage, marked today by enormous piles of broken offering pots. Now anyone of any substance who made offerings or even received burial near "the staircase of the Great God" at Abydos enjoyed eternity.

Bedouins bring tribute in this tomb painting of Khnumhotep II. The Khnumhotep

clan ("Khnum Is Content") was a remarkable provincial family at Beni Hasan,

who served as governors and court officials. Khnumhotep II had so many dealings

with Asians that he included them in his vision of the afterlife.

Many people had their mummies transported to Abydos by boat before interment to participate in the water festivals that commemorated the god.

The more democratic Osiris cult made funerary rites big business. A huge vocabulary of more than 1,100 incantations and spells came into use, often copied onto the interior surfaces of sarcophagi. They were seen to have magical effects. Proclaims one incantation: "As for any person who knows this spell, he will be like Re in the eastern sky, like Osiris in the netherworld." These so-called Coffin Texts also served as guidebooks to the underworld. In later times the sacred incantations were copied onto papyri and became the celebrated *Book of Going Forth by Day*, or *The Book of the Dead* of the New Kingdom. Anyone who could afford it could purchase such a papyrus, which could be ordered with any combination of spells one desired.

INVADERS OF OBSCURE RACE

The tradition of long Middle Kingdom reigns continued with Amenemhet III, who came to the throne about 1818 B.C. and presided over Egypt for 48 years. This pharaoh was a builder of temples and palaces on an enormous scale. He surrounded himself with an army of officials who supervised building projects, tax collection, agriculture, quarrying, and military expeditions. The reforms by Amenemhet's predecessors had created a strong centralized government run by men with diverse responsibilities. The stela of a high official named Sehetep-ib-re at Abydos waxes lyrical about his many responsibilities as "Grandee of the King of Lower Egypt." He described himself among other things as...

> ...overseer of horn, food, feather, scale, and pleasure ponds...Keeper of silver and gold....
> Master of secrets in the temples; overseer of all works of the king's house. More accurate than the plummet....
> An official who unravels what is knotty.

Even in death Amenemhet's officials protested their slavish loyalty. Sehetep-ib-re's stela adjures the onlooker to "cleave to His Majesty in your hearts," for...

> He is Re who sees with his rays, / Who lights the Two Lands more than the sun-disk, / Who makes verdant
> more than great Hapy [god of the Nile], / He has filled the Two Lands with life force.

For the first time since Snefru's day in the Old Kingdom the pharaoh built himself two pyramids. One rose an estimated 246 feet high at Dahshur; the second, about

DEATH IN THE PROVINCES

Between 1902 and 1904 British Egyptologist John Garstang excavated the provincial cemeteries at Beni Hasan in Middle Egypt. He cleared a staggering 888 tombs of 11th and 12th dynasty nomarchs, many lesser officials, and humbler folk. Cemeteries like Beni Hasan (above) reflected the social order of the day. The nomarchs occupied the upper levels of the necropolis area in rock-cut tombs with vestibules, offering chapels, and several chambers, some with columns, surrounded by people of lower social orders. Garstang's excavations produced a wealth of wooden models of granaries, boats, even butcher and carpentry shops, crammed into burial chambers, everything to maintain the life of the deceased in the otherworld: musical instruments and furniture, bows, arrows, mirrors, and ornaments of all kinds. Paintings adorned the richest tombs, like that of Khnumhotep II. Here the pharaoh hunts ducks in a papyrus marsh (left). His sepulchre tells us of Egypt's regular dealings with desert nomads and Asiatics who came to trade and graze their stock.

190 feet high at Hawara. In the end Amenemhet III was buried at Hawara in the heart of a mud-brick pyramid that was a maze of dead-end corridors, trap doors, and sliding panels to confuse potential tomb robbers. The builders carved out the burial chamber from a solid block of quartzite 23 feet by 8 feet by 6 feet high. This they sank into the ground before erecting the pyramid. The king and his daughter the Princess Neferu-Ptah were laid to rest inside the chamber, sealed with a 45-ton roofing slab. Despite all the precautions ingenious thieves managed to violate the tomb. Amenemhet had an enormous 1,000 foot by 800 foot mortuary temple built on the south side of the pyramid, described wonderingly by Herodotus and the Greek geographer Strabo as a maze of chambers and passages. Unfortunately little remained of this extraordinary building by the time Egyptologist Flinders Petrie excavated it in the late 19th century.

Amenemhet III was the last of the great Middle Kingdom pharaohs. After his death about 1770 B.C. Egypt entered on seemingly less prosperous times. His successor, Amenemhet IV, was short-lived and may have ruled with Queen Sobeknefru as co-regent. The century that followed saw a procession of 13th dynasty pharaohs ruling from Itjtawy. We know little of what was going on except for a suspicion that the Nile floods were capricious, with at least some periods of drought. The stronger kings maintained control over both Lower and Upper Egypt and still traded with Byblos, but there was a slow decline in artistic and technical standards. By 1700 B.C., the situation had deteriorated, perhaps as a result of the growing independence of Asian communities in the delta. Itjtawy must have been a whirlpool of political infighting. Power rotated between factions in the royal bureaucracy, which now threatened to absorb the throne that had created it.

Thousands of Asians had settled in the delta, many of them nomads fleeing from extended droughts in their homelands. Some were wandering Bedouins seeking sanctuary, trading wool and other products with Egypt, or simply buying emmer wheat and watering their flocks, a tradition that went back to the earliest times. Others stayed. Some became laborers in exchange for shelter and food; others were sold into slavery. Well aware of the importance of the delta as a gateway to Asia, Amenemhet I founded a royal domain with temple and settlement at Avaris on the then deepwater Pelusiac branch of the Nile in Lower Egypt. The ruins of Avaris lie near the modern village of Tell el-Daba in the eastern delta. For more than 20 years Manfred Bietak of the University of Vienna has uncovered the ancient city with meticulous excavations, tracing its history through many tumultuous centuries.

Avaris soon attracted a growing, and increasingly cosmopolitan, Canaanite

FOLLOWING PAGES: In a funerary stela in the Cairo Museum an 11th dynasty official named Inyotef and his wife Sithathor receive offerings for the deceased. Their beloved son, at bottom right, dedicates food to them, borne by estate servants at top right.

population. Many later inhabitants were soldiers, others traders from the Byblos region, as well as people engaged in turquoise mining in the Sinai. The port bustled with ships from Cyprus and the Levant, even from distant Crete, their weathered sails bringing them to the docks laden with clay amphorae and all manner of luxuries and raw materials. Porters off-loaded the heavy vessels with slings attached to their heads, setting them on donkeys, carrying them through the harbor gates to palace storerooms, or passing them to the crews of riverboats berthed nearby. Merchants in long robes bargained in the shade, fingering bales of fine linen or samples of lapis lazuli. Small children dodged among the cursing laborers, sniffing the exotic spice scents wafting from the ships, then trying to climb aboard, only to be cuffed by a watchful skipper.

Enormous quantities of imported clay vessels passed through the port. At least two million of them lie broken there. Many were amphorae holding olive oil and wine, long staples of the Egyptian trade. A 13th dynasty palace in the city contained fine Cretan pottery, artifacts from northern Syria, and an irrigated vineyard. Temples of Asian design stood in the city. Later the palace gardens became a cemetery for palace officials. Pairs of donkeys and sheep lie within the entrance pits of their tombs, a custom typical of a culture dependent on the caravan trade—and of Bronze Age communities in Syria and Palestine at the time. The cemeteries reveal that most of the city's male population came from the Levant whereas the women were local, a typical intermarriage pattern for mercenaries and sailors. At least a third of the population suffered from anemic diseases caused by parasites or from occasional malnutrition, which would have made them vulnerable to shipborne epidemics. Discounting the usual high infant mortality, mean life expectancy at Avaris was only 34.4 years for men and 29.7 years for women.

By the 13th dynasty Asiatics were common throughout the Nile Valley. They were expert brewers and vintners, weavers and seamstresses, dancers and doorkeepers. Many were little more than slaves, but others achieved positions of considerable responsibility, their sons and daughters taking Egyptian names and becoming absorbed in an increasingly diverse society. Desert folk were a familiar sight in Egyptian towns. A tomb painting at Beni Hasan in middle Egypt shows a group of Hikau khasut ("Rulers of Foreign Lands") in their brightly colored coats being received in audience by the nomarch Khnumhotep, governor of one of the Eastern Desert nomes during Senusret II's reign.

Cosmopolitan delta towns like Avaris saw a gradual influx of foreign mercenaries and merchants during the 12th and 13th dynasties. By 1800 B.C. they may have formed half the town's population. The machinery of government (Continued on page 164)

ARTISTRY WITH THE LOOM

A long established craft even in the time of ancient
Egypt, weaving dates back to the earliest farming
days. Egyptians almost invariably wove linen, for flax
was a staple crop. Every village, every family had its
weavers who fashioned clothing, sleeping mats, and
other articles for daily use. Nobles' estates staffed their
own textile shops with expert artisans, who turned
out the finest quality fabrics. Like everything else
in Egypt the technology was simple; output increased
by the application of more and more hands. The simplest looms were horizontal ground looms (left). Here
weavers at Qurna, near Thebes, weave sleeping mats with
the lengthways threads attached to pegs in the ground.
A wooden model shows the chancellor Meketre's weavers
working a horizontal loom (above). A row of workers
spin as a length of fine linen stretches across the loom.
Ancient Egyptian cloth has survived mostly as shrouds
and bandages for the dead. Only a few garments exist,
but they were generally plain, color having been added
by beaded nets, braids, and metal accoutrements.

in the south passed imperceptibly into foreign hands. Eventually Hikau khasut (usually known by the Greek corruption, "Hyksos") rulers quietly set up an independent dynasty in Avaris with a view to taking over the country, this while the pharaohs still presided over the rest of Egypt from Itjtawy upstream. After 1630 B.C. the Hyksos warlord Sheshi seized the ancient capital at Memphis and turned Avaris into a great stronghold.

Centuries later the Egyptian priest Manetho wrote depressingly of the massive invasion of foreigners who had flooded into the delta and set up their own state. "A blast of God smote us; and unexpectedly, from the regions of the East, invaders of obscure race marched in confidence of victory against our land. By main force they captured it without a blow." "The Hyksos invasion" duly passed into the annals of Egyptology but is probably a myth. An increasingly cosmopolitan world made itself felt in the north and changed Egypt forever. The growing economic and military power of the Hyksos and of Kerma, in Nubia, caused Egypt to fracture once again into two kingdoms—that ruled by the Asians and that of the old "Head of the South." Perhaps the Itjtawy court fled south to Thebes and set up shop in the heart of the southern vizierate.

THE HYKSOS INTERLUDE

For just over a century Hyksos kings reigned over Lower Egypt from Avaris. They must have won the loyalty of many Egyptian officials to do so and duly worshiped Re, the sun god of Heliopolis as well as Seth, even choosing Egyptian throne names. The Hyksos monarchs presided over the delta and the Nile Valley as far upstream as the Asyut region, maintaining an uneasy relationship with Theban rulers in Upper Egypt. They exercised considerable influence over much of Sinai and the Levant and opened Lower Egypt to new ideas from a shifting eastern Mediterranean world.

We know the Hyksos had direct contact with the Minoans, for a circular alabaster jar lid bearing the name of the second Hyksos king, Khyan, has been found at the Palace of Minos at Knossos near modern-day Heraklion in northern Crete.

The Upper Egyptians considered the Hyksos interlude an unmitigated disaster, a time when usurpers brought chaos to the Two Lands. But the Hyksos and their aggressive trading practices opened the Nile Valley to the innovations of a rapidly changing Bronze Age world. They brought bronze into general use, this metal being far more effective for tools and weapons than the softer copper of earlier times. They imported olive and pomegranate trees, an upright loom as well as innovative weaving methods, and new kinds of musical instruments, such as the lyre and tambourine. Also, Hyksos breeders brought into Egypt the first humpbacked Asian bulls to improve their stock.

Additionally, the Hyksos changed the military tactics of the region. Their armies relied on mobility and the deadly forces of archers armed with newly designed multipart bows. Daggers and swords came in more efficient designs. After some centuries generals introduced the horse-drawn chariot, of little use in the marshy delta but a vital strategic weapon in desert warfare. Theban generals fast realized the advantages of archers and chariots in open terrain and put them to good use in their campaigns against the Hyksos in Lower Egypt and Palestine.

Hyksos monarchs never ruled over Upper Egypt, but their Theban rivals were powerless to challenge their authority downstream. The Thebans presided over a strip of territory extending from the towns of Kusai and Abydos to Elephantine but not into Nubia, where the kingdom of Kush was in firm control. Thebans maintained their military strength by recruiting large numbers of Nubians as mercenaries. The Medjay warriors were light infantrymen who delighted in hand-to-hand combat. Once the Hyksos were defeated, the Medjay became the backbone of the pharaoh's police force. Many of them rose to high office. The two kingdoms adhered to an uneasy truce punctuated by border skirmishes in the hinterland between their domains.

In about 1570 B.C. the Hyksos king Apepi I wrote to his Theban contemporary Seqenenre, complaining that he was unable to sleep in his Avaris palace owing to the roaring of the hippopotamuses at Thebes, presumably a complaint about the militaristic ambitions of his southern neighbor. The roaring of the hippopotamuses erupted into open warfare after the Hyksos entered into a lucrative trading alliance with Kerma, using desert trade routes that skirted Theban domains.

THE KINGDOM OF KUSH

Kerma, upstream of the Third Cataract in what is now the Sudan, was an important settlement as early as the fourth millennium B.C. The village became a town, then a sprawling city, capital of the kingdom of Kush. The growing city straddled strategic trade routes from south to north and deep into the surrounding deserts. Kerma was a funnel for the gold, ivory, and slaves traded downstream. As Egypt fell into disarray, Kush's ambitious rulers expanded into Lower Nubia. The pharaoh's garrisons promptly changed sides and served new masters. Kush developed as a distinctively

A young servant girl carries offering jars on her head in the prosperous world of chancellor Meketre's tomb. A white linen sheath covered with a bead net adorns the wooden statue of the maiden. Her right hand, not shown, pinions a live duck.

Nubian state, selective in its adoption of Egyptian culture. Its rulers may have even employed some expatriate Egyptians as short-service officials and paid them in gold. Many of their people were familiar with Egypt at firsthand from having served in the military or police. But the state was distinctively African and cherished its independence over many centuries. Kush prospered by controlling the ancient trade routes that extended downstream to Egypt even in times of political turmoil.

By the time the Hyksos came to power in the far north, Kerma was a rich and powerful kingdom with a strong economy based on agriculture, cattle, and a growing gold trade with the north. Charles Bonnet of the University of Geneva has devoted his career to excavating the city, the earliest and largest in Africa outside Egypt. In its heyday during Hyksos times Kerma covered about 65 acres, a striking indigenous metropolis. Its ruler controlled all of Lower and Upper Nubia. He lived in the fortified city core, protected by massive 30-foot high mud-brick walls with four gateways and projecting, rectangular towers. A huge white temple (deffufa) rose high above the walls, its white pylons visible from miles away. This temple covered an area of 3,500 square feet, a large building even by pharaonic standards.

Superficially the deffufa resembled an Egyptian temple, but the interior reflected very different religious beliefs and also housed workshops for the production of prestige goods. Instead of having a front entrance, a side entrance and a stairway led to a small sacrificial chamber where goats and sheep were offered on a circular marble altar. Another stairway climbed to the roof where outdoor rituals, perhaps for the sun god, were once performed. A 16-foot mud-brick wall surrounded the religious precincts, enclosing not only the deffufa but small shrines and living quarters for the priests. Perhaps 2,000 people lived within the larger fortifications, in the royal palace, and in dwellings of the nobility.

Kerma's ruler originally held audience in a large circular hut with mud-brick walls that stood to a height of at least 30 feet. A conical thatched roof covered the structure, later abandoned in favor of a rectangular mud-brick palace with an imposing audience hall where the ruler sat on a dias to conduct official business. A great deal of trading activity centered on this large complex, aligned with the main temple entrance. The ruler's public appearances were carefully orchestrated. The palace had large storage chambers and an archive room, where Bonnet unearthed thousands of clay seal blanks used to mark goods or to close messages.

Kerma was a sprawling city, a walled community surrounded by clusters of much smaller settlements. The central precincts housed a diverse population, not only the ruler

MOVERS OF WATER

The Middle Kingdom pharaohs never forgot the great famines at the end of the Old Kingdom, spending lavishly to build grain-storage facilities and major irrigation works (left). Starting with Amenemhet II, the pharaohs realized the great agricultural potential of the Faiyum depression west of the Nile. Thousands of workers deepened and widened a natural watercourse, now called Bahr Yusef, which joined the depression to the Nile. Settlements sprang up, such as a rectangular town of brick buildings for quarriers working basalt outcrops at the northwestern edge of the Faiyum. Pharaoh Amenemhet II built his pyramid (now no more than a mud-brick mound) at Dahshur, east of Snefru's much earlier 4th dynasty Bent Pyramid and closer to the Faiyum than other possible sites. Amenemhet III, who reigned for about 48 years and devoted energy to the Faiyum, built a pyramid at Hawara, even closer to the depression. The corridorlike entrance (above), west of center on the south side, led to a maze of passages and chambers to deceive looters—without success.

Lake Qarun, west of the Nile, glistens at sunset. Runoff from Amenemhet III's vast irrigation works formed the lake, which lies below sea level. Middle Kingdom agricultural schemes accelerated the transformation of the Faiyum depression into an organized oasis, dramatically increasing the nation's grain production.

and his family and court but also officials, soldiers, and a hierarchy of priests, as well as a large population of commoners, most of whom lived outside the city walls. Artisans here were expert in gold and ivory and created some of the finest clay vessels ever made in Africa: red and black colored and of eggshell thinness. The city's houses reflect a complex, wealthy society, with many two-room dwellings fronted by a courtyard and others with more complicated ground plans. Vast enclosures between the city and the river housed enormous numbers of animals stored for food. Excavators have even found the imprints of cattle hooves in the soil! Small villages once flourished along now dry Nile channels in the hinterland around the capital. They grew grain for Kerma and stored it in special structures with raised wooden floors.

The vast Kerma cemetery about two miles east of the city provides a fascinating window into Nubian society of the day. More than 30,000 people lie there. Commoners were buried with few possessions. Wealthier members of society lay on well-made wooden beds provided with a box of personal possessions such as bronze razors and stone vessels for eye pigment or ointment. They wore linen and leather garments, occasionally caps decorated with mica ornaments. Four exceptionally large royal burial mounds with mud-brick mortuary shrines lie along the southern edge of the cemetery. Averaging about 290 feet across, the mounds once housed the corpse of an unknown ruler laid out in all its finery on a magnificent bed. Lavish supplies of locally made inlaid furniture, weapons, and pottery accompanied each ruler. The mourners lined the area outside the burial chamber with statues and statuettes of Egyptian pharaohs and officials plundered from abandoned fortress towns and cemeteries under Nubian control.

On the day of the funeral large crowds gathered at the great burial mound where narrow corridors led to the burial chamber. A long procession of mourners walked to the tomb carrying offerings amidst great wailing and chanting. Trusted priests and officials closed the doors of the burial chamber. The ruler's attendants, his entire harem in their best finery, their children, and dozens of slaves filed into the earthen passageway and crowded tightly together close to the burial chamber. Excavator George Reisner tells the tale: "The cries and all movements cease. The signal is given. The crowd of people assembled for the feast, now waiting ready, cast the earth from their baskets upon the still but living victims...and rush away for more. The frantic confusion and haste of the multitude is easy to imagine." Death came quickly to many of the victims, who pressed their hands over their faces or their heads between their elbows. "At that last moment we know from their attitudes in death that a rustle of fear passed between them and that in some cases there was a

spasm of physical agony." Having filled the passageway and buried the mourners alive, the crowd enjoyed a great feast of oxen that had been slaughtered to accompany the dead lord.

Sophisticated merchants and politicians, the princes of Kush kept a firm pulse on political events downstream in Egypt. They were careful to develop their own alliances with the Hyksos, which did not endear them to the lords of Thebes. Their delta trade avoided Upper Egypt by passing along desert routes like the Alamat Tal, which linked oases all the way to downstream of the great Qena Bend of the Nile.

The Thebans responded to the Hyksos–Kerma alliance by patrolling the most used tracks and erecting watchtowers, two of which survive at the Theban end of the Alamat Tal track. Desert patrol units prowled along the trails, intercepting donkey caravans at night and slaughtering Hyksos traders. University of Chicago archaeologists John and Deborah Darnell have surveyed many of these tracks, which are littered with potsherds from centuries of Egyptian history. They have identified caravan stops where travelers left graffiti on the rocks, many of them prayers to the gods, a commemoration of a special journey, or the names and titles of the policemen who patrolled the routes. There are even inscriptions from about 1800 B.C. in what may prove to be an early phonetic alphabet.

Hor, the 14th king of the 13th dynasty (ca 1720 B.C.) reigned only a short time.

The life-size wooden statue with flashing eyes shows King Hor unclothed, with

the upraised hands of his ka on his shoulders (not shown in image).

THEBES TRIUMPHS

Thebes became bolder. And the city's rulers proclaimed themselves true pharaohs. In about 1543 B.C. the Theban lord Ta'o II attacked the Hyksos in several bloody engagements. Ta'o II himself led at least one of these expeditions and fell under a rain of missiles. His mummy, preserved in a cache of royal burials at Deir el-Bahri, shows that he was attacked by at least two people who assailed him with a dagger, ax, spear, and perhaps a club. The king was lying down at the time, for his mortal wounds are horizontal. His body was hastily embalmed without the usual care, then transported to Thebes for burial.

Ta'o II's son Kamose found himself controlling Upper Egypt and part of the Nile's middle reaches while the Hyksos controlled the north. His generals advised caution, but Kamose decided to attack his enemies without warning. His armies pressed northward, employing the same kind of sophisticated chariots and weapons as used by the enemy. They new weaponry proved so effective in open terrain that the depiction of a pharaoh riding in a chariot in victory against his Asian and Nubian enemies became commonplace on the walls of temples and palaces. The Hyksos monarch Apepi wrote to the ruler of Kush begging him to launch an attack against the Theban rear. "Come, navigate downstream, do not be afraid...for I will not let him go until you have arrived." The two rulers would then divide the spoils. Unfortunately for Apepi the messenger carrying the letter was intercepted by a Theban desert patrol.

Kamose reigned for only three years. His brother Ahmose I came to the throne about 1539 while still a young boy. The formidable Queen Aa-hotep served as co-regent in the early years of his reign. The pharaoh resumed the Hyksos campaign about halfway through his 25-year reign. He led a series of attacks against Memphis, Avaris, and other Hyksos-fortified towns. The Hyksos were a stubborn foe, but the relentless pressure from the south wore them down. A long inscription in the tomb of a doughty warrior named Ahmose, son of Ebana, takes up the story. The veteran soldier served in many fierce campaigns against the Hyksos under Ahmose, Amenhotep I, and Thutmose I. When the pharaoh laid siege to Avaris and fought three battles there, Ahmose (the soldier) "took captive there one man and three women, total four heads, and His Majesty gave them to me for slaves." After bitter fighting and the complete destruction of Avaris, Ahmose's armies chased the Hyksos into Palestine and laid siege to the town of Sharuhen, their stronghold in southern Palestine. At the end of it all Ahmose the Theban reigned supreme over a ravaged but reunified Egypt, soon to become a mighty imperial power.

Four colossal seated figures of Ramses II tower over the facade of his rock-cut Abu Simbel temple in Nubia. A symbol of all-powerful Egypt, Ramses II dwarfs the standing members of his family and the god Amun-Re above the entrance. From inside the shrine, figures of gods peer out eternally.

IMPERIAL EGYPT

The mortuary temple of King Seti I outside the Valley of Kings epitomizes the power of New Kingdom pharaohs. Ahmose, Amenhotep III, Seti I, Ramses II—the names of the mightiest New Kingdom monarchs are a litany of greatness. King Ahmose and his successors expelled the Hyksos and turned Egypt into a great imperial power. Egypt became a major player in the swirling politics of the eastern Mediterranean where the great powers of the day vied for control of strategic ports and markets. At home the pharaohs were militaristic leaders who turned Nubia into a colony and grew rich on its gold. They lavished wealth on the temples of the god Amun-Re at Thebes and dazzled ally and enemy alike with their wealth. The brief reign of the heretic pharaoh, Akhenaten, was but a hiccup in Egypt's five centuries of supreme greatness. After 1200 B.C., the stable conditions on the country's frontiers deteriorated. Palace intrigues and civil unrest weakened the state. By 1100 B.C., Egypt had become two countries with the pharaoh ruling in the north and the high priests of Thebes controlling the south.

Dynasty 18

Ahmose
Amenhotep I
Thutmose I
Thutmose II
Queen Hatshepsut
Thutmose III
Amenhotep II
Thutmose IV
Amenhotep III
Akhenaten
(Amenhotep IV)
Smenkhkare
Queen Ankhetkheprure
Tutankhamun
Aye
Horemheb

Dynasty 19

Ramses I
Seti I
Ramses II
Merneptah
Seti II/Amenmesse
Siptah
Queen Tawosret

Dynasty 20

Sethnakhte
Ramses III
Ramses IV
Ramses V
Ramses VI
Ramses VII
Ramses VIII
Ramses IX
Ramses X
Ramses XI

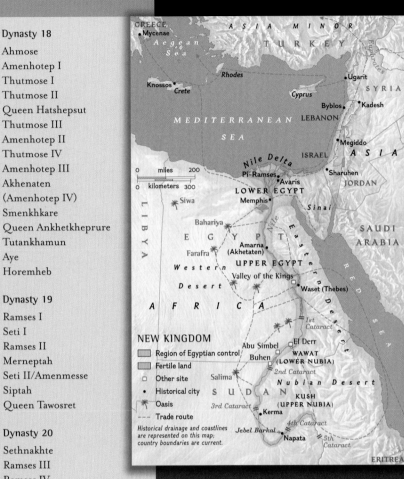

NEW KINGDOM

Region of Egyptian control
Fertile land
□ Other site
• Historical city
✳ Oasis
--- Trade route

*Historical drainage and coastlines
are represented on this map;
country boundaries are current.*

"The crew commander Ahmose son of Ebana, the justified...I let you know what favors came to me. I have been rewarded with gold seven times in the sight of the whole land, with male and female slaves as well...."

I have always fantasized about sitting down for a long talk with Ahmose son of Ebana in his old age. The old soldier must have been walking history. He served three pharaohs, witnessed the defeat of the Hyksos, was present at the ravaging of the Hyksos capital of Avaris in the delta and Sharuhen in Asia, and fought in several bloody Nubian campaigns. He died honored and respected, his deeds remembered on the walls of his sepulchre: "The name of the brave man is in that which he has done; it will not perish in the land forever."

The Pharaoh Ahmose valued his battle-hardened regiments, which brought him to power and kept him there. Fresh from the slaughter at Sharuhen, the victorious Theban king turned his attention to Nubia,

The death mask of Yuya gazes with the confidence of wealth and power (opposite). A military man, a Master of Horse, Chancellor of the North, and father of Queen Tiye (wife of Amenhotep III), Yuya served two pharaohs—Thutmose IV and Amenhotep III. A scarab and the ram-headed sun god (above) appear in the Litany of Re scene on the walls of Pharaoh Seti II's tomb.

Ahmose son of Ebana at his side. "Now when his majesty had slain the nomads of Asia, he sailed south . . . to destroy the Nubian Bowmen. His majesty made a great slaughter among them, and I brought spoil from there: two living men and three hands. Then I was rewarded with gold once again, and two female slaves were given to me. His majesty journeyed north, his heart rejoicing in valor and victory. He had conquered southerners and northerners."

King Ahmose was a survivor, as much at home on the battlefield as in a palace. He mastered battle tactics that used chariots and archers, which allowed him to adopt strategies of attack rather than defense, leaving his enemies constantly off balance. Such tactics worked well against the Hyksos, who were no mean fighters themselves. The pharaoh could never let his guard down against a foe with superb connections in all corners of the eastern Mediterranean world. To counter any possible threats, Ahmose and his successors extended the frontiers of Egypt across the Sinai and far into Asia, also southward deep into Nubia. The great kings of earlier times had conquered and received tribute from submissive foreign lords. The new rulers of the Nile combined conquest with colonization, and they Egyptianized Nubia. For the first time Egypt became an ambitious imperial power, deeply engaged in the affairs of the larger Mediterranean world.

THE BULL-LEAPERS OF AVARIS

King Ahmose took no chances in the strategically vulnerable delta. He rebuilt Avaris as a heavily defended fortress. The new town rose on the ruins of the Hyksos capital. A huge mud-brick platform with a riverside gate gave a magnificent view over the Pelusiac branch of the Nile, at that time a deepwater channel to the sea. Military barracks, several temples, storerooms, and a palace for the pharaoh once existed inside the walls of the city. Unfortunately ancient builders quarried away the abandoned structures many centuries ago, leaving a gigantic archaeological jigsaw puzzle behind them. Instead of excavating buildings, Austrian Egyptologist Manfred Bietak and his colleagues have spent years dissecting huge piles of mud brick and wall plaster—with astounding results.

Construction rubble makes for unrewarding excavation under the best of circumstances. Avaris was no exception until Bietak unearthed hundreds of lime wall-plaster fragments adorned with paintings executed in Minoan style. The Cretan motifs and style of the wall paintings are unmistakable—a bearded priest, acrobats, river landscapes, and craggy mountains like those of Crete, unknown in Egypt. Such scenes are not unique. Cretan wall paintings occur in other Bronze Age cities in the Levant, as Cretan kings sent artists abroad as tokens of favor to important trading partners. But only the Avaris palace boasts bull-leaping scenes. One frieze shows bulls, bull-leapers, and others cavorting against a labyrinthine background characteristic of Cretan palace art. A bull charges, his face turned toward the artist. The bull-leaper grasps the beast around the neck, his legs in the air. Another bull lunges nearby, but this time the acrobat has fallen off the animal.

Why would friezes in Cretan style be painted on the walls of an Egyptian palace? The explanation may lie not in Egypt but in Crete. A century ago archaeologist Arthur Evans excavated the so-called Palace of Minos at Knossos in northern Crete and revealed the hitherto unknown Minoan civilization to an astonished scholarly world. The palace was a labyrinth of courts and rooms, many adorned with magnificent wall paintings of people and bulls.

Evans reconstructed some of the friezes, somewhat imaginatively according to his critics. Goddesses and priestesses, processions, bulls, mythic animals, and lions, even waving grass and flowers: The Knossos art is lively and highly distinctive. The most famous scenes depict acrobats jumping over fierce bulls, twisting and turning in the air as they cavort with the charging animals. Despite extended search no one had ever found bull-leapers anywhere else until they turned up at Avaris. They were unique to the Western Court at Knossos, the greatest Minoan palace ever built.

Manfred Bietak believes the Avaris friezes depict the distant Western Court. Avaris and Knossos share other royal art and symbolism too—depictions of mythical griffins and felines, animals at the summit of nature's hierarchy. At Knossos griffins protected goddesses and queens. Maybe they did at Avaris as well. Bietak wonders if a diplomatic marriage between the Egyptian and Knossos royal families might not be involved. Ahmose is known to have married two of his sisters but may have had a Cretan wife as well; we do not yet know. Perhaps Ahmose, having bested the Hyksos, feared a surprise attack by land and sea. The Minoans were the best seafarers of the day so the pharaoh may have cut a deal with the lord of Knossos—protection of sea-lanes in exchange for access to Egyptian ports and her abundant gold. We know that Minoan trade delegations were soon familiar sights at the Egyptian court. They appear in art on the walls of Theban nobles' tombs.

Avaris was a fortress and a palace compound for the victorious pharaoh, a base for his campaigns in western Asia. Here troops could rest while their officers kept a close eye on Egypt's northeastern frontier. Here, too, Ahmose could embark his invading armies for a quick coastal passage to the strategic ports of the Levant. For centuries Avaris remained a meeting place between Egypt and the eastern Mediterranean world. Polyglot crowds of artisans, seamen, and traders thronged the quays and streets of the city. Perhaps the dockyard was Penu-nefer (Happy Journey), the famed harbor in Lower Egypt once thought to lie at Memphis, upstream. Just under three centuries later Avaris became the port for Ramses II's royal residence at nearby Pi-Ramses and thrived as a vital link to the outside world.

Ahmose was well aware of the economic and strategic importance of his fortress. He realized only too well that the key to his power lay in consolidated, expanded frontiers, close political ties with potential rivals, and complete control of Nubian trade. Whether the pharaoh's officials liked it or not, Egypt had become part of what today we would call a global economy. A vast web of economic and political interconnectedness linked the Nile with the Levant, with copper-rich Cyprus, with Asia Minor, Mesopotamia, and the Aegean Islands. The ancient world was joined economically

Sunrise breaks over the Valley of the Kings, viewed from the summit of el-Qurn.

Thutmose I started the custom of royal burial in the Valley of the Kings,

a custom that was to endure for five centuries. Generations of Egyptologists

have searched for rock-cut sepulchres in the valley, which has still not yielded

all its mysteries. So far dozens of elaborate tombs have been located.

and politically as never before—and Egypt was an important part of it. Her products and raw materials, her ideas, knowledge, and religious beliefs were carried far and wide by ship, on the backs of donkeys and people, and by her armies. Soon New Kingdom Egypt achieved wealth and power unrivaled in earlier times.

The eastern Mediterranean world was a cockpit of competing rivalries, constant minor wars, and diplomatic maneuvering between states and empires large and small. Everyone vied for a piece of the lucrative trade funneled through Byblos, Ugarit, and other wealthy Levantine ports. When Ahmose came to the throne, the Hittite kings ruled over present-day Turkey, their ambitious eyes resting on nearby lands in what we now call Syria.

The seafaring Minoans of Crete controlled a huge trade in olive oil, timber, and wine from the Aegean to the Syrian coast and the Nile. The kingdom of Mitanni on the Euphrates River vied with the Babylonians and Hittites. The political equation in Asia was a quicksand of alliances and broken promises. Pharaoh after pharaoh made diplomatic marriages with Asian royal families and exchanged rich gifts, bribed rulers of strategic cities with gold, and fought throughout the Levant. Their survival depended upon their military and diplomatic skills.

SECURING THE NUBIAN BOWMEN

The short-reigning Pharaoh Kamose in the 17th dynasty, who ruled prior to Ahmose, had campaigned in Lower Nubia, presumably to counter any possible threat of an invasion from the south as he attacked the Hyksos. He encountered little resistance. The kingdom of Kush kept to itself during the northern wars that followed. Ahmose I did not turn his attention to Nubia until the 22nd year of his reign. Then he marched south, slaughtering large numbers of Nubians and rehabilitating some long-abandoned garrisons. His successor Amenhotep I led another expedition south when "his Majesty smote that Nubian Bowman in the midst of his army." The ubiquitous Ahmose son of Ebana records how the prisoners were "carried off in fetters, none missing, the fleeing destroyed as if they had never been." Ahmose was rewarded with gold and slaves and given the title "Warrior of the Ruler."

Things were quiet until about 1491 B.C., the second year of Thutmose I's short reign, when rebellion and unrest threatened the security of trade routes. Thutmose was an older man who married the daughter of Ahmose the Liberator. An experienced

On the wall of the tomb of Pharaoh Amenhotep II, the solar bark bearing the ram-headed sun god sails through the underworld. A goddess holds back Amun-Re's enemy, the giant snake Apophis, to allow safe passage of the royal boat. Artists created a visible underworld in the tombs of deceased pharaohs as a map to ensure safe and successful passage through the afterlife.

soldier, he marked his tenure by a series of brilliant military campaigns in Nubia. He sailed southward with a large fleet. Again Ahmose son of Ebana was present, this time promoted to crew commander for his prowess in towing a boat through turbulent rapids. The Egyptians encountered little resistance, since most of the garrisons seem to have quietly changed sides, as they had done when the Nubians took over a century before. The only stand came at Buhen where the Nubians resisted fiercely.

Excavator Walter Emery unearthed thousands of Kerman pot fragments in the rooms of the burned and sacked fortress. "His majesty became enraged like a leopard. His majesty shot and his first arrow pierced the chest of that foe." One can imagine the heat and choking dust, the swarms of arrows shot at close range with deadly effect. Men clasp arrow shafts in their chests and bleed to death. Others turn and run, only to be felled by showers of missiles in the back. Then come the fierce war cries of the charioteers and the drumming of hooves as the pharaoh orders a charge into the churning Nubian regiments. As the Egyptians count their casualties and round up hundreds of prisoners, vultures circle overhead.

From a newly established fort at Tombos, Thutmose subsequently attacked Kerma and made his way into the heart of Nubia as far upstream as the Fourth Cataract. The royal expedition lasted a year and was a triumph for the now formidable Egyptian army, much of it Medjay recruits from the Eastern Desert. Thutmose sailed north laden with booty, with the rebel leader's body pinned head downward on the ship's bow.

The Egyptians now garrisoned Upper Nubia permanently to ensure that the river trade flowed uninterruptedly northward. As for Thutmose, he campaigned successfully in Asia as far as the banks of the Euphrates River where he set up a boundary stela.

GREATEST OF HEAVEN, ELDEST OF EARTH

At home the 18th dynasty pharaohs tightened their grip on the land. They placed a great deal of responsibility in the hands of local governors but also retained Egypt's standing army in the interests of maintaining law and order. To the pharaohs war was an inevitable answer to enemy provocation, the age-old "smiting of the foes," and a discrete lever of power at home. They presided over an increasingly militaristic state where the king was revered as a living god, also as a brave warrior, victorious in battle.

Victories were excellent propaganda. So was prowess in battle. The New Kingdom

pharaohs reminded everyone of their bravery at every turn. In about 1420 B.C., Amenhotep II boasted of how he had completed successful target practice in his "northern garden," where "he found erected for him four targets of Asiatic copper, of one palm in thickness, with a distance of twenty cubits between one post and the next." The king rode past them in his chariot, shooting on the move, and hit every one.

Every pharaoh paid careful attention to his regiments and to the gods. The army was no longer a provincial responsibility but came under the control of the central government. Military service became a respected profession. The pharaohs relied heavily on both native Egyptians and well-paid mercenaries, rewarding them with generous shares of booty, land grants, and other incentives. Standardized training, especially of charioteers, became the norm.

Close ties developed between the pharaoh and his army, to the point where the ruler built a network of political allies around him at court. Many of them were the sons of foreign leaders—some sent to strengthen ties; others taken as hostages and educated at court. They first became war comrades of the king, then moved on to high official positions. In this way the pharaoh developed his own direct contacts within the conservative and often slow-moving bureaucracy.

The king was also careful to pay profound respect to the sun god Amun-Re. So rich were Amun's temples and estates that his priests became a powerful, sometimes even dominant, presence in the affairs of state. Thebes, or Waset, was the center of political administration for the south. She was a sacred city where the most important religious festivals associated with the divine monarchy unfolded each year. Poetry of the day celebrated the city's vital importance as "the pattern for every city. Both water and earth were within her from the beginning of time. . . . So mankind came into being within her, with the purpose of founding every city in her proper name. For all are called 'City' after the example of Thebes." Above all Thebes was the city of Amun.

"The Greatest of Heaven, Eldest of Earth," Amun was one of the most ancient deities of Egypt, mentioned in Old Kingdom pyramid texts and long associated with Thebes. As the Theban pharaohs tightened their grip on Egypt, their divine patron also assumed ever greater prestige. Ahmose the Liberator showered Amun's temples with gifts in thanksgiving for his victories. His successors adorned and remodeled the god's temples at Luxor and Karnak. They made a point of attending the lavish festivals that punctuated the holy year.

Amun's name means "hidden." He was "unknowable," described in a theological document composed in the reign of the great Pharaoh Ramses II as "hidden from the gods, and his aspect is unknown. . . . No god knows his true appearance. . . . No one testifies to him accurately. He is too secret to uncover his awesomeness, he is too great to investigate, too powerful to know." He became the greatest of all the gods, a deity who was above all the created world. Amun's unknowable qualities distinguished him from the other gods, who had roles in nature. He was the supreme cause, the divine whose perceptive utterances created nature through the agency of Ptah, the chief deity of Memphis. All other Egyptian creator gods became manifestations of Amun: "All the gods are three: Amun, the Sun, and Ptah, without their seconds. His identity is hidden as Amun, his face is the sun, his body is Ptah."

Although he himself may have been unknowable, Amun most frequently appears as a man crowned with two tall plumes. He was sometimes known as "Lord of the Thrones of the Two Lands," or as "King of the gods." As Amun-Re he became as one with the sun god Re. Amun-Re symbolizes the transcendence of Amun and his very presence in the sun. The doctrine of his transcendence flowered during the New Kingdom when the great temples at Karnak and Luxor became the center of the state's religion.

FOLLOWING PAGES: The obelisks of Thutmose I and Queen Hatshepsut tower over the Great Temple of Amun at Karnak, part of the largest single temple complex ever built. Generations of pharaohs lavished wealth on Ipet-isut, "the Most Select of Places" and rebuilt the temple to glorify Amun and their own deeds.

Amun's "cathedral" was the ancient temple at Karnak at the northern edge of the city. Pharaoh Thutmose I boasted of how he remodeled and restored the temple under the supervision of his architect Ineni and took care to record: "I made the boundaries of Egypt as far as that which the sun encircles. . . . I made Egypt the superior of every land." Amun became the imperial god of an imperial Egyptian state.

The Great Temple complex of Amun at Karnak, the largest temple ever built, was adorned and rebuilt by generations of pharaohs. The Egyptians called it Ipet-isut, "the most select of places," the place where Amun had his compound and Great Temple with the enclosure of his consort Mut immediately to the south and that of Montu, the original falcon god of the Thebans, to the north.

The temple lay along north-south (Nile) and east-west (sun) axes, following the more-or-less standard plan of a pylon entrance leading to an open court, then to a magnificent hypostyle hall. One of ancient Egypt's masterpieces, the hall is a forest of huge columns depicting the celestial realm of the sky supported above the Earth. The 134 columns, each about 79 feet high, of the hypostyle represent the dense marshland vegetation that sprang up around the primordial mound of creation—depicted by the temple's inner shrine. On a winter's late afternoon the sun's long rays filter between the columns, giving the effect of sun-dappled trees.

Victorian traveler Amelia Edwards aptly compared the columns to a dense grove of California redwoods. The hall leads to the sanctuary, the heart of the temple, the innermost chamber of the god's home. Amun's shrine was constructed of hard stone, protected by metal-clad wooden doors, and considered to be part of heaven on Earth. Only the pharaoh and the highest ranks of Amun's priesthood could enter the space where the god's image stood. Wrote Pharaoh Amenhotep III of Karnak: "Its pillars reach heaven like the four pillars of heaven."

Once each year in the second month of the inundation, the great god Amun-Re of Karnak visited his shrine at Luxor, one-and-a-quarter miles upstream. In "Opet of the South," the god visited the Amun who resided in the temple there. In procession the priests carried statues of Amun, his wife Mut, and their son Khonsu in sacred barks on their shoulders, the statues covered by discreet curtains. Huge crowds greeted the procession as it emerged from the temple.

People knelt or cheered, musicians played, dancers performed for the gods. At intervals the gods would stop to rest at specially built chapels where offerings were provided. Sometimes a petitioner would step out in front of the divine bark and beg for

a judgment from the god. If the god agreed, the procession would halt and the petitioner would pose his question. If the bark moved forward, the answer was yes; if backward, no.

At Luxor the noise rose to a crescendo. The god halted at a shrine outside the temple. Royal family members and other dignitaries greeted him with offerings and sacrifices. Next Amun moved to shrines within the temple where elaborate rituals unfolded.He visited a kind of special version of himself in order to be rejuvenated. Symbolic wedding ceremonies reemphasized the divine parentage of the pharaoh. During the climax of Opet the pharaoh entered Amun's shrine accompanied by his priests. There in the dark, incense-laden chamber, he merged anew with his ka. Dramatically he then reappeared in public, miraculously transformed into a divine being, the "foremost of all the living kas." The gods returned in triumph to Karnak, this time by river, accompanied by the pharaoh in his royal barge.

Opet was a carefully staged spectacle with the holy family of an Egypt emerging in public and the king present in person to absorb some of the power of the god. The festival reinforced the ties between the Egyptians and the gods which inhabited their cosmos. Opet was so important that the original 11-day festival had been extended to 20 days by the end of the New Kingdom. Karnak and Luxor provided the spectacular settings for the all-important rituals that validated the power and authority of the pharaoh. Interestingly, today's Thebans, on exactly the same day as Opet once began, celebrate a festival dedicated to two devout sheiks. One is buried in a mosque built within Luxor Temple; the other, near Karnak. The festival includes a big procession from Karnak to Luxor and even includes the carrying of boats—just like the transport of the divine statue on boats from ancient Egypt!

The Opet festival required the personal presence of the king even if he dwelt in Memphis to the north. His journeys to and from Thebes became a royal progress during Akhet, the season of inundation. Each night he stopped in a different town, where the local mayor had the task of feeding the king and his court. No pharaoh missed Opet, for the merging of the king with Amun had vital importance for Egypt. Opet symbolized continuity, the long thrust of history. The festival was a pageant; an exercise in royal legitimacy; a synthesis between myth, ancient ritual, architecture, and sheer display. Even a usurper pharaoh could be absorbed by Opet. General Horemheb, who came to the throne in about 1319 B.C., celebrated his coronation by combining it with Opet, legitimizing his claim to the throne with the precedents of history.

QUEEN HATSHEPSUT BECOMES KING

Thutmose I died in about 1485 B.C. His two oldest sons had already died, so the throne passed to his young third son, Thutmose II, the son of a minor wife. The court married him to his half-sister Hatshepsut, the eldest daughter of Thutmose I. Husband and wife reigned together until the pharaoh died in his early thirties, having prosecuted successful military campaigns in Nubia and Syria. The dying king may have realized just how ambitious his wife was. He carefully named his only son his successor as Thutmose III. The choice may not have been popular with many factions at court, for the young pharaoh was born of a harem girl named Isis. Inevitably Hatshepsut acted as co-regent with the new king with the support of high court officials. Whether this was due to her naked ambition or a matter of political necessity is unknown. If it was a political move, the circumstances must have been very unusual, for it was rare for a woman to become the personification of the male Horus.

The court architect Ineni records how Hatshepsut "settled the affairs of the Two Lands by reason of her plans. Egypt was made to labor with bowed head for her, the excellent seed of the god." With brilliant political opportunism she manipulated the Amun cult at Karnak, arranging for herself to be publicly selected as the next monarch during the Opet festival. In her famous Red Temple in the precincts at Karnak, Hatshepsut commissioned inscriptions that told how Amun had prophesied her ascent to the throne "through a very great oracle...proclaiming for me the kingship of the Two Lands, Upper and Lower Egypt." Undoubtedly this was propaganda rather than a choice made by people in a state of excitement during a major religious festival.

Hatshepsut was careful to select titles that legitimized her rule. She assumed the titles of the female Horus Wosretkau and Khnemetamun Hatshepsut, "She who embraces Amun, the foremost of women." At first she was depicted as a woman; but as time went on, her official portraits and sculptures show her in the full regalia of male kingship.

As the queen strengthened her hold on the reins of government, she commissioned her spectacular mortuary temple set in the natural amphitheater of cliffs at Deir el-Bahri. The inscriptions there make great play of her being crowned pharaoh before the court in the presence of her father, Thutmose I. According to the inscription the king chose the first day of the new year as the auspicious day of her crowning. The entire scene, including the alleged support of her father, was brazen fiction and an exercise in public relations. Here she commemorated her accomplishments, especially her famous expedition to the Land of Punt. Reliefs on the portico of the

EGYPT'S POWERFUL FEMALE KING

Queen Hatshepsut declared herself pharaoh in 1473 B.C.
An ambitious woman, she assumed all the male titles
and attire of the king's office and ruled for 15 years.
Hatshepsut selected the natural amphitheater of Deir
el-Bahri's cliffs for her mortuary temple, Djeser-dje-
seru, "sacred of sacreds" (right). Now partially
reconstructed, the sacred of sacreds took 15 years to
build. Visitors approached from the Nile along a 121-
foot-wide, sphinx-lined causeway, which led to now
vanished pylons. The temple itself rises in three courts
separated in colonnades, linked by ascending ramps.
The walls of the temple depict the marshes of Lower
Egypt and the quarrying and transport of great red
obelisks in Upper Egypt. The portico of the second
court tells the story of the queen's expedition to the
Land of Punt, a region on the Red Sea in modern-day
Eritrea or Somalia. In one relief the King and Queen of
Punt (above) receive the visitors, who returned bearing
precious metals and plants, including myrrh trees.

The cartouche-shaped, red granite sarcophagus (opposite, bottom) of Pharaoh
Thutmose III, one of Egypt's greatest warrior kings (opposite, top right), lies in his
burial chamber. Painted excerpts from the *Book of the Dead,* cover the walls like
scrolls. In a painting ravaged by tourists, Thutmose feeds from the tree of life.

temple's second court show the expedition setting off down the Red Sea and its arrival
in Punt, complete with the elderly ruler of Punt, Perehu, and his large queen Eti,
accompanied by her donkey. His courtiers carry gifts for the Egyptian expedition
leader, Panehsy. We see the ships of the expedition being loaded with sacks of myrrh
resin and myrrh trees, their root balls protected by baskets. Men carry ebony, gold,
ivory, incense woods, and leopard skins. Apes, dogs, and local people with their children crowd aboard for the journey northward. The Egyptians paid for their rich cargo
with glass beads, bangles, and weapons. Weeks later the expedition reaches Thebes in
triumph. Hatshepsut dedicates large heaps of myrrh to Amun.

Throughout Hatshepsut's reign Thutmose III at least nominally ruled alongside
her. He may have spent much of his time with the army, for the queen was no military campaigner. The years were well spent. When the queen died in about 1458 B.C.
after a reign of 15 years, Thutmose assumed his rightful throne. He immediately set
out under the banner of Amun to resecure the eastern frontier in the face of chal-
lenges from Asian princes. Thutmose was a decisive general. His army marched from
the Nile to Gaza across the desert in ten days, took the city, then advanced on the fortress
of Megiddo, which had rebelled against Egyptian rule. He decided to approach the
city walls through a narrow defile instead of a more obvious route. His officers warned
him about possible ambushes, but Thutmose boldly trekked through the dangerous
wadi at the head of his troops. The move caught the Megiddans by complete surprise
and divided their army in two.

The pharaoh joined battle next day. Thutmose "set out in a chariot of fine gold,
decked in his shining armor like strong-armed Horus." The Megiddans were routed
and fled for the city "with faces of fear, abandoning their horses, their chariots of gold
and silver, so as to be hoisted up into the town by pulling at their garments." Many
barely escaped with their lives, hauled up the walls by their clothes as the gates closed.
Foolishly the Egyptians paused to loot instead of pressing their advantage. Megiddo
had time to strengthen its fortifications and fell only after a seven-month siege. Meanwhile Thutmose subdued the surrounding territory. "The princes of this foreign land
came on their bellies to kiss the ground to the might of his majesty," and brought lavish tribute with them. Not for nothing did the American Egyptologist James Breasted
call Thutmose III "the Napoleon of Ancient Egypt."

For the next 18 years Thutmose launched summer campaigns against Syrian
cities, often ferrying his army from the Nile by sea. At the end of these campaigns the

important city of Kadesh and more than 350 lesser strongholds and towns were in Egyptian hands. Much of the spoil from the pharaoh's campaigns went to adorn the already magnificent shrines at Karnak. Young foreign princes were brought to Egypt as hostages, educated in Egyptian ways, then sent home to become obedient vassals.

During the last dozen or so years of his reign the pharaoh could rest on his laurels, knowing that his kingdom was secure and its Asian and Nubian frontiers at their greatest extent. Thutmose III reigned in great splendor surrounded by wealthy and highly competent officials. The government of the kingdom depended entirely on the efficiency and goodwill of the king's officials—and ultimately on the decisive example set by the monarch himself. The tomb of Thutmose's vizier Rekhmire preserves the speech delivered by the pharaoh at his installation—the theme: dedication and responsibility:

> *He is the copper that shields the gold of his master's house.... / He is not one who bends his face to*
> *magistrates and councillors, / Not one who makes of anyone his client.... / The whole land is eager*
> *for [counsel of the vizier]; / See to it that all is done according to law, / That all is done exactly right, /*
> *In [giving a man] his vindication.*

Thutmose presided over a prosperous kingdom until his death. His son Amenhotep II assumed the throne in about 1426 B.C. and moved swiftly to quell uprisings in Syria. In the third year of his reign he turned against rebellious Nubian chiefs, executed seven captive chieftains, and hung them upside down from the prow of his ship. Six were strung up in Amun-Re's temple at Karnak, the seventh at the Nubian town of Napata "in order to cause to be seen the victorious might of His Majesty for ever and ever." The kingdom was now at peace, Egypt's frontiers in good order. His successor, Thutmose IV, came to the throne about 1400 and cemented a treaty with Egypt's great Asian rival, the kingdom of Mitanni, on the Euphrates River, by marrying a daughter of its ruler. In 1390 the throne passed to his son by one of his chief wives, Mutemwiya. Amenhotep III was between ten and twelve years old.

THE DAZZLING SUN DISK

The Egyptians explained a royal birth as a sexual union between the pharaoh's mother and Amun, who temporarily assumed the form of her husband. The Birth Room at Luxor commemorates the birth of Amenhotep III. "When he [Amun] had transformed himself into the Majesty of this husband, King of Upper

FOLLOWING PAGES: The famous solar court of the Great Temple of Amun at Luxor, created by Amenhotep III, was the pharaoh's favorite temple, his place of ceremonial rejuvenation. He lavished wealth on the shrine, built a multiroom complex at the southern end, and completed the masterpiece that is this court.

and Lower Egypt...he found her as she was resting in the beauty of her palace. She awoke on account of the aroma of the god... He went to her straightaway...and he caused her to see him in his form of a god.... She rejoiced at the sight of his beauty, and love of him coursed through her limbs.... Words spoken by Amun-Re, lord of the thrones of the Two Lands, before her: 'Amenhotep, ruler of Thebes, is the name of this child I have placed in your body.... He shall rule the Two Lands like Re forever.'" This was the moment at which the royal ka was formed, the invisible and immortal life force that came to the pharaoh from his royal ancestors and from the beginnings of time.

The new pharaoh married a woman of nonroyal rank named Tiye, the daughter of a noble couple, Yuya and Tuya. By the fifth year of his reign he was campaigning against rebellious chiefs. Boastful stelae tell of the king's bravery, he the "fierce-eyed lion whose claws seized vile Kush, who trampled down all its chiefs in their valleys." The usual kingly rhetoric, of course, as was talk of his prowess as a mighty hunter. Even as a teenager Amenhotep III loved to hunt. Hundreds of soldiers corralled wild bulls, elephants, or lions inside huge enclosures. Then Amenhotep would ride forth in his chariot in full hunting regalia, drawn by magnificent horses, shooting at the captive beasts with arrows and javelins. The slaughter was impressive. A commemorative scarab duly records: "His Majesty proceeded against all these wild bulls. The number thereof: 170 wild bulls. The number His Majesty took in hunting on this day: 56 wild bulls." No less than 123 such scarabs tell us Amenhotep killed 102 lions "with his own arrows" in the first decade of his reign. Everything was carefully calculated to portray a divine ruler, a great warrior, and an unerring hunter, triumphant against the forces of chaos and evil. The king himself ordered the issue of hundreds of carved scarabs through-out the kingdom recording his deeds as a young man.

Amenhotep called himself the Dazzling Sun Disk. Official ideology proclaimed him master of the world from Mycenae to Babylon and depicted him trampling on captives and foes. Such grandiloquent dreams suited the mood of the day, but Egypt's foreign relations were much more complex. She was now a cosmopolitan country as never before, with the power and wealth to occupy a dominant position in the eastern Mediterranean world. Amenhotep was a master diplomat, a genius at flattery, the strategic use of lavish gifts, and political marriages. He bribed, he cajoled, he threatened, he promised gold, then withheld it. The great pharaoh understood the intricate balance of power that maintained peace between the ambitious states surrounding the eastern Mediterranean and had the military force (Continued on page 202)

PHARAOH LARGER THAN LIFE

One of Egypt's greatest pharaohs (above), Amenhotep III, the Dazzling Sun Disk, was master of diplomatic and political intrigue. He used gold and royal marriages as the currency of international relations. The mortuary temple of Pharaoh Amenhotep (left) on the west bank of the Nile, across from Luxor Temple, reflected his love of extravagant statements and lavish display. Two 65-foot-high sandstone statues of Amenhotep stood before the entrance, all that now remains of a once stupendous building. After an earthquake in 27 B.C., Greek and Roman travelers flocked to hear one of the figures emit a bell-like sound caused by the expanding stone at sunrise. Repairs by Emperor Septimius Severus silenced it forever. Each summer the inundation left only the inner sanctuary, on a small knoll, clear of the water. This annual flood eventually destroyed the temple.

and dazzling wealth to back his word. In a world where public display meant everything, Egyptian pharaohs had few rivals.

About 1887 some peasants unearthed a cache of crumbling clay tablets at the city
of Amarna, the royal capital of Amenhotep's successor, his son Akhenaten. No one
knows how many cuneiform-inscribed tablets from the pharaoh's archives were lost
in their finding. About 350 diplomatic letters inscribed on the tablets testify to Amenhotep's genius at foreign relations.

It is as if we are sitting at his elbow as he wages diplomatic war with clay tablets.
We see him negotiating political marriages with promises of gold from Egypt's seemingly inexhaustible supply—the currency of her power. We learn that by the tenth year
of his reign he had already married the daughter of King Tushratta of Mitanni, thereby
cementing his father's alliance with an ancient rival. This strategic move kept the
aggressive Hittites at bay on the far side of the Taurus Mountains and gave Egypt a valu-
able ally in the Fertile Crescent.

Amenhotep was an inveterate marrier. Subsequently he bargained for the Mitanni
princess's niece, two Babylonian princesses, and the daughter of the King of Arzawa.
King Kadashman-Enlil of Babylon was reluctant. He complained that the pharaoh

Amarna, the capital city during Akhenaten's reign, was a showpiece for the worship

of Aten. Akhenaten's architects chose a riverside site backed by a ring of cliffs.

The city extended about eight miles along the Nile. Temples and major public

buildings occupied the center of the semicircle described by the cliffs. The Royal

Road joining the palace and city center ran parallel to the river.

"put my chariots amid the chariots of the *hazanu* [minor Syrian and Palestinian kings]: You caused them to be brought to the presence of the country [all] alike, in order that they be not seen separately." He complained that his sister, married to the pharaoh 20 years earlier, was mixed in with the other wives in the harem. "Is she really my sister...? My messengers did not recognize her...." The pharaoh frostily replied that she was well but that the King's ambassadors had been "nobodies," who did not deserve audience. To the Egyptians the Babylonian royal wife was simply the sister of a foreign vassal, one of the king's gifts. Whatever the diplomatic frictions, Egyptian ideology dictated that pacified enemies bow down to the pharaoh.

On another occasion the king of Babylon asked for the hand of a pharaoh's daughter. "From time immemorial no daughter of a king of Egy[pt] is given to anyone," came the firm reply. Babylon protested, but to no avail. No Egyptian princess would become a diplomatic tool.

Amenhotep used gold as the currency of peace treaties. He well knew of his rivals' insatiable lust for the yellow metal. Assuruballit, King of Assyria, wrote flatteringly: "Gold in your country is like dirt; one simply gathers it up. Why are you so sparing of it? I am building a new palace. Send me as much gold as is required for its adornment." He was bitterly disappointed when the promised gift fell far short of his expectations. Amenhotep deployed gold with calculated finesse. On one occasion he promised his father-in-law King Tushratta of Mitanni two solid gold statues but sent two gold-plated images instead. Tushratta was furious and continued to request gifts of gold "that has never been worked." Every diplomatic exchange of importance was accompanied by flattery and lavish gifts of jewelry and other exotica. Tushratta once sent "10 teams of horses; 10 wooden chariots along with everything belonging to them; and 30 women and men." Bridal dowries in gold and kind amounted to hundreds of thousands of dollars in modern currency and were part of the expense of doing diplomatic business. Amenhotep bought peace with gold and princesses.

Few pharaohs expended so much time and money on display. In the 30th year of his reign Amenhotep celebrated with a Heb-sed ceremony at Thebes on a scale unimagined for centuries, the first of three during his reign. He commissioned scores of life-size statues of himself throughout the kingdom. He handed out spectacular gifts to his trusted advisers amidst much celebration and feasting. News of the festivities traveled as far as Babylon, prompting the king to complain that "when you celebrated a great festival, you did not send...to me, saying 'Come, eat and drink.'"

The Heb-sed was the culmination of years of building and public works. Amen-hotep spent lavishly on Karnak and commissioned massive remodeling at Amun's Luxor Temple, the king's "place of justification, in which he is rejuvenated: the palace from which he sets out in joy at the moment of his Appearance, his transformations visible to all." He built himself a huge mortuary temple opposite Thebes, which was quarried and washed away in the next dynasty. Only two huge statues of the pharaoh remain, known incorrectly for two thousand years as the Colossi of Memnon (named by classical writers after a legendary Ethiopian prince who fought at Homeric Troy).

The Dazzling Sun died in 1353 in the 37th year of his reign. He was buried in a magnificent sepulchre in the Valley of the Kings. His wife Tiye survived for at least another decade and resided in the capital of her second son, Akhenaten, at Amarna.

THE HERETIC PHARAOH

Genius, heretic, madman—history has no shortage of epithets for Amenhotep's son Amenhotep IV. Why did he abandon the worship of Egypt's traditional gods in favor of a single solar deity Aten? Why did he change his name to Akhenaten and abruptly move his capital to a new site midway between Memphis and Thebes? Did these acts result from religious fervor, careful political calculation, or sheer eccentric whim?

Early on in his reign Akhenaten erected four new temples within the precincts of Karnak, but they were dedicated not to Amun-Re but to the solar disk, Aten, which must have caused consternation among the priesthood of the sun god. The ideological shift continued. In the fifth year of his reign the king abruptly changed his name from Amenhotep ("Amun is content") to Akhenaten ("One who serves Aten"). The change stemmed from his seemingly heretical preoccupation not with the hundreds of traditional Egyptian gods but with what he considered the supreme force of all—the light of the sun, which gave the Earth life every day. A famous inscription depicts Akhenaten worshipping Aten (light), the sun rays pouring down on Earth, each ending in a hand proffering an ankh, the hieroglyph for "life."

Aten was nothing new for he had been venerated during the Old Kingdom as a minor aspect of the sun god. But Akhenaten worshiped the Aten in its own right as a divine force accessible only by the pharaoh, thereby eliminating the need for a priesthood. The tomb of Akhenaten's chief minister Aye displays a hymn to Aten, said

Queen Nefertiti presents a magnificent pose of aristocratic serenity. The German

Egyptologist Ludwig Borchardt found this masterpiece in a storehouse attached

to the Amarna workshop of the sculptor Thutmose, "overseer of works and sculptor"

to Pharaoh Akhenaten. More than 20 prototype plaster casts of royalty and others

came from this workshop.

to have been written by the king himself: "Thou arisest fair in the horizon of Heaven, O Living Aten, Beginner of life . . . there is none who knows thee save thy son Akhenaten. Thou hast made him wise in thy plans and thy power." In his sepulchre Aye says that the king himself gave him instruction in the new doctrine. No one knows why Akhenaten pursued his unconventional beliefs. Some scholars believe he started a genuine intellectual revolution, the first in recorded history. Others think he was trying to reduce the political power of the priests of Amun in Thebes, something his father had also attempted with little success.

Akhenaten also changed established artistic conventions. A stela commemorating Bek, Akhenaten's chief sculptor and master of works, tells us that the king himself instructed the court sculptors to adopt a new, more informal style. The artists responded brilliantly with a new convention for royalty. They depicted Akhenaten with an elongated face, a long chin, and large head perched atop a long neck. He was fat in unusual places around the thighs, buttocks, and breasts and walked on spindly legs. Generations of Egyptologists, puzzled by his strange appearance, have attributed it to chronic disease or have even wondered if Akhenaten was androgynous. Most likely the Amarna art style conveyed a relaxed sensualism that was soon emulated by the king's courtiers. Bek carved himself in the likeness of the pharaoh with pendulous breasts and belly.

This more naturalistic art style may have been an attempt to depict kingship as something different and outside the normal plane of human existence. Akhenaten thought of himself as the earthly agent of the Aten, the source of the divine force for humanity. So pictures of him and his family in informal poses were probably not intended to propagate family values but, rather, to perpetuate the image of the king as supreme god of all life. He described himself constantly as he "who lives on truth," implying he alone understood the true revelation of the divine. Amarna art style has a refreshing and often charming naturalism quite unlike anything before or after it.

Queen Nefertiti ("the beautiful one has come") is, after Ramses II and Tutankhamun, probably the best known of all ancient Egyptians. The world-famous bust of her, now in the Berlin Museum, portrays a classic beauty. She appears frequently in official art, especially on the walls of Aten's temple at Karnak, where she is even seen smiting a captive with a club, hardly the act of a submissive wife. She bore the pharaoh six daughters. Her second daughter Meketaten died in about year 12 of Akhenaten's reign. The grief-struck parents are seen beside her supine body in a relief in the royal tomb.

At first Akhenaten tolerated the traditional gods. He must have encountered such strong opposition that he resorted to draconian measures. He outlawed Amun, closed the god's great temples at Thebes, and took over their revenues. Amun's name was erased from public buildings and monuments. The pharaoh also abruptly moved the royal capital to a virgin site at Amarna midway between the traditional capital at Memphis and the religious capital at Thebes. The name of the new city and short-lived capital was Akhetaten, or "the horizon of Aten." The abandoned remains lie close to the surface, uncluttered by the debris of later cities—a boon for archaeologists.

The king chose a natural amphitheater of cliffs for Amarna, marking the boundaries with 15 large carved stelae inscribed in the rock, showing the pharaoh adoring Aten with his family. Aten had guided the king to this place, they tell us, a location associated with no other deity.

A year later Akhenaten returned on a second visit and caused more inscriptions to be carved into the cliffs. "The area within these four tablets . . . belongs to Aten my father: mountains, deserts, meadows, islands, high ground and low ground, water, villages, men, animals, and all things which Aten my father shall bring into existence eternally and forever." He also vowed to be buried near the city precincts. The pharaoh had his new city designed and quickly built, unfettered by the traditions of the past. It sprawled over an area of about eight by three miles, including much farmland, with an estimated population of more than 20,000 people. He himself lived in the North City in a massively fortified palace. The royal precincts also housed an administrative building and a huge commodities warehouse.

A processional route formed the backbone of Akhetaten. The so-called Royal Road ran from the North City past the palace of the king's eldest princess Meritaten to the Central City where the Great Palace stood, with brightly painted halls, courtyards, and pavements.

This may have been the place where the king received foreign delegations and held official functions. The pharaoh himself sat under carefully placed shades, but the foreign dignitaries were obliged to stand for long hours in the hot sun. Assyrian King Assuruballit I wrote a stern letter of complaint to Akhenaten on the subject: "Why are my envoys kept standing out in the open sun? They will die out in the open sun. If it does the king good to stand in the open sun, then let him stand out in the open sun himself and let him die for himself."

A brick bridge over the Royal Road linked the official buildings with a small working palace with a Window of Appearance, where the pharaoh would appear in public.

FOLLOWING PAGES: Bathed in the sun's rays, Akhenaten and his wife Nefertiti play with their children. At left, Akhenaten lifts his daughter Meritaten for a kiss. Ankhesenpaaten rests against Nefertiti's shoulder. Meanwhile Meketaten, dandled on her mother's knee, looks at Nefertiti and gestures to her father.

Small offices, among them the official archives, the "Bureau of the Correspondence of the Pharaoh," sprawled around the palace. The great temple of Aten and another small temple to the same deity lay nearby with open courts and altars that brought the worship of Aten into the open, unlike the closed shrines of Karnak and Luxor. On major festival days hundreds of altars sent columns of sweet-smelling incense smoke and the more acrid smell of burnt offerings into the blue sky where the Aten watched over all, casting life-giving rays on the populace. The king himself, the nation's all-powerful intermediary with the sun, oversaw the festivities.

Everything at Amarna served the sun god and his living representative on Earth. The pharaoh and his family lived in grand isolation in the North City, emerging on formal occasions to descend in splendor on the palaces and temples of the central precincts. Akhenaten and Nefertiti rode forth in state in their brilliantly decorated chariots, the royal bodyguard "headed by the chief of police of Akhenaten, Mahu" running crouched alongside them. Such moments of royal progress were very different from those of the god Amun's barks that had traveled the processional way at Thebes. At Amarna the king himself rode before his people in his role as a divine ruler. Many of his formal audiences stressed how dependent the court was upon him. The pharaoh was a dazzling sight in his glittering regalia.

Tomb reliefs tell us that the pharaoh would reward high officials at his Window of Appearance before a formal courtyard. The person to be honored entered the king's presence down an avenue of trees in a courtyard. A scribe would recite the official's titles, old and new, perhaps describe some of his deeds, as the honoree made deep obeisance, his forehead touching the ground seven times. The courtier Pennifer proudly commissioned a tomb relief showing Akhenaten bestowing him with gold necklaces, as minor officials and scribes pack other gifts in a chest. Royal servants bring forth amphorae of oil and wine and baskets of other useful commodities as the ceremony unfolds and other officials await their turn.

The city itself was a series of neighborhoods, described by Egyptologist Barry Kemp: "The king and his entourage recede into the background, and icons are the main reminders of his presence. In the larger houses we see officials living...the good life of private income and state donation...dividing their time between their city house and their family home in the provinces, writing letters and making visits to keep in contact. In the small houses crowd a range of people of lower status—some servants, others holders of minor office, many making things for sale.... Busy people, idle people,...some desperate and many harassed people." (Continued on page 214)

THE GOOD LIFE IN AMARNA

For 1,500 years Egyptian royal art changed but little. Kings, queens, and nobles wore aloof, perfect faces. But Akhenaten encouraged more naturalistic styles and the use of bright colors. The royal family enjoyed pride of place in the art, showing affection, posing with their children or with favored nobles. Scenes even depict the king and queen grieving at the death of their daughter Meketaten—never a subject in prior royal artistic tradition. Akhenaten himself often appeared with elongated face, long ears, and full lips, shown here bearing an offering tray. Polychrome glass containers, such as the fish-shaped bottle for carrying unguents, indicate that Amarna was one of the great glassmaking centers of the day. A grape cluster made of beads assembled on wire once adorned a building. An alabaster drinking cup, shaped and hollowed with copper and bronze tools and sand abrasives, bears Akhenaten's name. The art of Amarna eternally testifies to its good life.

While Akhenaten pursued his god, his two chief officials, Aye (perhaps his father in-law) and General Horemheb, ruled a country that was showing some signs of strain. Both these closely related officials were later to become pharaoh. They somehow managed to keep the lid on political and religious dissent while bending simultaneously with the changing political winds at court. They commanded the loyalty of the bureaucracy but conformed, like all the pharaoh's courtiers, to the new beliefs even if the conformity was skin deep. Cherished religious artifacts in Amarna's houses tells us that many commoners at Akhetaten still followed some of the ancient beliefs. The same may have been true throughout the country although the major temples were closed and the priesthood was inactive.

Akhenaten's experiment failed. We do not know how much the populace supported his revolutionary ideas. They had been taught to believe that life began with a series of well-known, oft-recited cosmic events—the appearance of the primordial mound in the midst of dark waters, the birth of Osiris, and so on. Human life and the familiar world of ma'at were consequences of these mythic happenings. The new religious world was perhaps unfathomable, even frightening. Aten was an impersonal god, impossible to depict in any way other than by a disk or a hieroglyph. Traditional gods like Amun were more anthropomorphic, beings easier for people to relate to, who appeared briefly at public ceremonies. The pharaoh may have perceived the irrelevance of much religious thought of the time and replaced it with a simple concept of a solar disk. But the worship of Aten created political unrest. Akhenaten's visions of a new cosmos perished shortly after his death and became little more than an uncomfortable memory.

Most of the time Akhenaten occupied himself with religious devotions and his new capital. In foreign affairs he tried to minimize the costs of his empire while attempting to curb the power of the Hittites. The strategic alliance with Mitanni fell apart, despite urgent pleas from King Tushratta. Egypt's loyal vassals near the frontier sent desperate requests for assistance against aggressive rebels and menacing Hittite kings, which Akhenaten ignored. Hittite emissaries flattered the Egyptian court while their armies overran Mitanni and Tushratta was assassinated. Some of Egypt's allies transferred their loyalties to the growing Hittite presence in the interests of survival. Otherwise Akhenaten allowed his vassals to bicker among each other to prevent their uniting against Egyptian rule. He also permitted the kingdom of Amurru, in modern-day Syria, to expand as a buffer zone between Egypt and the growing power of the Hittites. He seems to have avoided a major military campaign, perhaps because he needed troops at home to maintain internal security.

Egypt was in serious disarray when Akhenaten died about 1336 B.C., sometime after the grape harvest, probably in the 17th year of his reign. Archaeologists dispute the details of what happened next. It is thought that two pharaohs ruled during the four years that passed before Prince Tutankhaten took his place on the throne. The young king, likely a son of Akhenaten, was only ten years old but was already married to his half-sister Ankhesenpaaten, Nefertiti's oldest daughter. This marriage brought him the support of the main branch of the royal family and assured him the succession at a time of intense political intrigue. He also had the backing of the two most important high officials in the kingdom—Aye, commander of chariotry and fanbearer at the king's right hand, and Horemheb, a general and capable administrator. Horemheb's titles reveal his amazingly broad responsibilities: "Overseer of Generals of the Lord of the Two Lands," "King's Deputy in Every Place," and most important of all "Hereditary Prince of Southern and Northern Egypt," a title intended to mark him as his master's designated successor. We know nothing of the relationship between Aye and Horemheb, but they must have had a common interest in restoring order and

A marvelous piece of furniture, this: A gold and silver inlaid throne from Tutankhamun's tomb. The young king rests in a chair inside a floral pavilion open to the rays of the life-giving sun. Queen Ankhesenamun, wearing a fine linen dress, anoints his shoulder with perfume.

the old ways. The two may well have quietly brokered a deal that made Horemheb the eventual successor in the event that their young master produced no heir.

These two remarkable men effectively ran Egypt for Tutankhaten and lost no time in restoring religious orthodoxy. Just over a year after assuming the throne, Tutankhaten changed his name to Tutankhamun, while his wife became Ankhesenamun. His advisers moved the court back to Memphis. The pharaoh issued a proclamation from the ancient palace of Thutmose I reciting his traditional titles and announcing his performance of traditional benefactions for "his [divine] father and all the gods . . . having repaired all that was ruined . . . and having repelled disorder throughout the Two Lands." One sees the not-too-subtle hands of Aye and Horemheb behind the king's sudden largesse to Amun and Ptah, the restoration of local cults, and the refurbishing of temples. They gave Tutankhamun the ancient title Repeater of Births, which signaled the dawning of a new age.

The young king had been on the throne for nine years when the Egyptians attacked the strategic town of Kadesh, in the Levant, which had rebelled against the pharaoh's rule with Hittite encouragement. The attack failed. Hittite King Suppiluliumas I promptly defeated the Hurrians of northern Syria and consolidated his hold over Egypt's former domains in the north. At this critical moment Tutankhamun died.

Tutankhamun expired suddenly at about age 20. He would have been just a footnote in history were it not for the discovery of his virtually undisturbed tomb by Lord Carnarvon and Howard Carter in the Valley of the Kings in 1922. The discovery enthralled the world, but the cause of his death remains an intriguing mystery. X-rays have revealed a small sliver of bone deep within the king's brain cavity, perhaps the result of a blow to the head. Did the king fall from a chariot? Was he killed in battle? Or did a rival faction at court simply murder him? All we know is that Tutankhamun's death came as a complete surprise, so much so that he was buried in a small tomb that some think was originally dug for the elderly Aye. Many of the objects in the tomb came from the state's funerary store, including at least one of the king's coffins, which bears different features. Even the quartzite sarcophagus was secondhand, the surface hastily recut to remove the original names.

The king's early death left Ankhesenamun in a difficult position. She was childless and surrounded by older, ambitious men. She may be the queen who took the unprecedented step of writing a letter to Hittite King Suppiluliumas I, asking him to send one of his sons for her to marry, thereby securing the succession.

"Never will I take a servant of mine and make him my husband," the woman wrote, in an obvious reference to Aye and General Horemheb. Suppululiumas was astonished. "Nothing like this ever happened to me in my entire life," he exclaimed. He sent messengers to check on her story, then dispatched his son Prince Zannanza as a prospective husband. The Prince was murdered or died of plague on the way and never reached Memphis.

For all his honorific titles Horemheb was in no position to assume the throne. He was preoccupied with the war in Syria and may have been out of the country. A powerful faction at court favored the aged Aye, who is seen in Tutankhamun's burial chamber wearing a royal crown as he performs the ancient ceremony of Opening of the Mouth at the funeral. Horemheb stayed in the background for the brief four years of Aye's reign, then claimed the throne as his right after Aye's death about 1319.

Horemheb was a complete pragmatist of great experience. Over his 30-year reign he completed the task of restoring the prestige of Amun but took the precaution of appointing priests from the army to curb earlier excesses. Karnak was rebuilt and Akhenaten's Aten temples torn down, the stones used as filling for a new temple pylon. (During modern restoration, a brilliant feat of archaeological research, thousands of these blocks came to light and have been pieced together with computers to reconstruct the Amarna scenes depicted on them.) Horemheb systematically removed any traces of his Amarna predecessors from public monuments. He even went so far as to place himself officially next in line after the beloved Amenhotep III. The ex-general maintained control over the military by dividing the army into two large units, one in the north and one in the south. His goal was nothing less than to create the foundations for a new age, this time a military kingdom. In this he was successful.

THE GOOD HERDSMAN WHO SUSTAINS HIS TROOPS

Horemheb failed to produce an heir, so the throne passed for two years to his close confidante Ramses I, a career army officer whose family came from the northwest delta area of Avaris. His son Seti I—like his father a former vizier and troop commander—succeeded to the throne about 1290 B.C. As was the case with his immediate predecessors, Seti's power came from prowess at war. He maintained close ties with the army and married within military circles, taking as his wife Tuya, the daughter of an officer. They had four children. The oldest, a boy, died while still

FOLLOWING PAGES: Tutankhamun's gilt coffin and granite sarcophagus lie in his burial chamber in the Valley of the Kings. On the walls, hastily executed paintings show the vizier Aye as pharaoh performing the Opening of the Mouth for Tutankhamun, a ceremony that legitimized his rule.

young; a daughter, Tia, and a younger son, Ramses, survived to adulthood. The youngest daughter, Henutmire, was born much later and eventually became a minor queen of her older brother, who succeeded his father as Ramses II.

Seti's well-preserved mummy shows a man of striking appearance and great resolution. Ever restless and a born soldier, Seti saw it as his divine mission to restore the glorious days of Thutmose III and Amenhotep III. Like Tutankhamun he assumed the title "Repeater of Births" to symbolize Egypt's rebirth and a new era of greatness.

The pharaoh's energy was remarkable. In the first year of his reign he emulated Thutmose with a rapid advance across the Gaza Strip, thereby securing his supply routes to coastal ports from attack. Seti then overwhelmed several fortress cities. Inscriptions show large numbers of prisoners being slain in Amun's presence. In later campaigns Egyptians met Hittites in battle in Lebanon and were successful in battle. A relief at Karnak shows Seti's army capturing the fortress of Kadesh from Hittite defenders, a town that would assume great symbolic and other importance in Ramses II's reign.

Seti, of all pharaohs, earned his honorific title: "the good herdsman who sustains his troops." On an inspection of gold-mine country in the Eastern Desert near Edfu, the king noted the difficulties of the desert journey and ordered a watering station and a well dug for the gold caravans that passed that way. "It is full of water in great quantity," he boasted. Seti built a temple nearby, complete with scenes of his victories over Asian and Nubian foes, and even appointed a special group of gold-washers to provide a supply of the precious metal for the temple in perpetuity.

The well project was a modest one by Seti's standards, who commissioned public works on an unprecedented scale. He chronicled his victories at Karnak, where his architects and artisans labored over the great hypostyle hall, one of the masterpieces of Egyptian art with 134 gigantic columns depicting the primordial papyrus marsh. At Abydos Seti commissioned another masterpiece, a temple to Osiris that commemorated his devotion to this most popular of all Egyptian deities. The temple, with its seven sanctuaries to the major gods, included one dedicated to the now deified king, who died during the temple's construction. The main hall bears reliefs showing the pharaoh as high priest carrying out the daily rituals for the gods.

A hall of records is of particular interest to Egyptologists; it shows Seti and his son Ramses before the official lists of all Egypt's pharaohs from the earliest times, thereby linking them with the origins of Egyptian monarchy. (Continued on page 226)

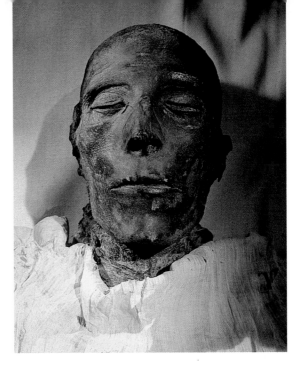

SEPULCHRE OF SETI I

Pharaoh Seti I (ca 1290-1279 B.C.), formerly vizier and
troop commander, was buried, after a 11-year reign,
in an elaborate tomb in the Valley of the Kings—one
of the longest, deepest, and finest of all the royal tombs
there. Circus strongman turned adventurer Giovanni
Belzoni, who discovered the sepulchre in October 1817,
copied the magnificent paintings and exhibited them
in London along with the king's alabaster sarcophagus.
The painted corridors of Seti's tomb descend steeply
more than 300 feet below ground to a vaulted burial
chamber where the king lay (left). Astronomical texts
adorn the upper half of the vault, while constellations
flanked by deities appear on the lower tiers. Scenes
from the *Book of the Dead* and other sacred texts cover
the walls. The wooden barrier, foreground, leads to
a passage that descends below the chamber, perhaps
a symbolic route to the primordial waters far beneath.
The king, one of the best preserved of all royal mummies (above), retains to this day an aura of authority.

On royal instructions, the scribes omitted any mention of Hatshepsut or of the Amarna pharaohs. The list jumps directly from Amenhotep III to Horemheb. Some administrative documents even go so far as to describe Akhenaten's reign as "in the times of the Enemy."

In the desert behind one Abydos temple the king built a structure known as the Osireion, entered through a long tunnel bearing painted scenes, images from the *Book of Gates* of journeying through the underworld. The passage opens into a huge 100-by-65-foot hall, where the body of Seti lay with all its funerary paraphernalia before burial in the Valley of the Kings. The building was underground and included a central mound surrounded by water, which commemorated the origins of the Egyptian world in the primeval waters.

Seti's ultimate masterpiece was his tomb in the Valley of the Kings, perhaps the most elaborate of all Egyptian royal tombs. Virtually all the New Kingdom pharaohs, starting with Thutmose I, were buried in rock-cut tombs in what is now called Wadi Biban el-Muluk, an arid valley in the shadow of el-Qurn, a pyramidlike hill sacred to the goddess Hathor. Why Thutmose and his successors chose this location remains a mystery, but the valley known to the Egyptians as "the Great Place," lay under what can be called a symbolic pyramid close to Thebes, the sacred city of Amun. New Kingdom monarchs were buried in subterranean chambers with hidden entrances designed to foil even the most determined of grave robbers. Here they lay in mind-boggling splendor, surrounded by their lavish possessions and all the material comforts needed for eternity, their ornately carved sarcophagi and coffins rich in gold and jewels. The aromatic oils and unguents buried with them were worth fortunes; the gold in their tombs beyond avarice. The tomb of Tutankhamun, hastily constructed and furnished, gives us a tantalizing glimpse—although partially looted—of the extraordinary riches that must have accompanied Seti I and other great, longer-lived kings into eternity.

Giovanni Belzoni, a circus strongman who had turned to treasure seeking, discovered Seti I's tomb in October 1817. He entered through a narrow staircase, followed a downward-sloping corridor adorned with brilliant paintings, bridged a shaft designed to foil looters and drain off floodwater, and penetrated a false wall that hid a decoy burial chamber. Then he descended though a concealed entrance down another stairway and corridor into a pillared antechamber and then into the actual chamber, more than 300 feet below the ground. Seti's magnificent translucent alabaster sarcophagus still lay there, its lid smashed by the ancient robbers, who had long preceded Belzoni.

Magnificent paintings on the tomb walls depict the Litany of Re and scenes of the king in the presence of the gods. The lower passages show the Opening of the Mouth ceremony; the ceiling of the burial chamber carries the heavens and its constellations, astronomical texts, and a row of deities.

For all their precautions the dead pharaohs' tombs were soon looted. There was so much wealth underground that robbers deemed the risks of detection acceptable. By a fortunate set of circumstances Seti's mummy has survived the millennia. Dockets on the mummy record that it was restored, first during the time of Herihor, a former general and high priest of Amun (ca 1085 to 1079 B.C.), presumably after the tomb was robbed, then again about 20 years later. In desperation the priests moved a large cache of royal mummies, including that of Seti, to a deep cleft in the cliffs at Deir el-Bahri where they remained safely hidden until 1881. In that year some exceptionally fine antiquities came on the black market in Thebes. The authorities investigated and suspicion fell on the Rasul family. They were questioned and beaten, denied all knowledge of the finds, and were released. But the family quarreled among themselves over shares of the loot, and Abdul Rasul went to Thebes and confessed. He led archaeologist Emile Brugsch to an inconspicuous defile in the cliffs on the west bank. Brugsch was lowered into the darkness on a rope, where his candle lantern shone on an extraordinary vault of pharaohs. Wrote antiquities official Gaston Maspero: "And what Pharaohs! Perhaps the most illustrious in the history of Egypt, Thutmose III and Seti I, Ahmose the Liberator and Ramses the Conqueror.... I still wonder if I am not dreaming when I see and touch what were the bodies of so many personages of whom we expected to know no more than the names." Three hundred men were pressed into service to recover the mummies and load them onto a Nile steamer. As the precious cargo departed for Cairo, wailing women followed the boat, and men fired off their rifles in honor of the ancient monarchs. Back in Cairo, archaeologists unwrapped some of the mummies and gazed on the countenances of Seti I and Ramses II, more than 3,000 years after they had passed into the afterlife.

THE PLACE OF TRUTH

By Seti's time the building of royal tombs was a highly organized process. Only the very best artisans and artists labored in the Valley of the Kings, part of a permanent labor force who did nothing but work on royal sepulchres.

PRIVILEGED WORKERS

Deir el-Medina sprawls across the desert near the
Valley of the Kings (left). Necropolis workers and their
families made their home here. Whereas pharaonic
tombs primarily held religious texts, the artisans'
graves on the hillside above the village exhibit exquisite paintings of everyday life. For example, the artisan
Sennudjem plows the fields of the mythical afterworld,
accompanied by his wife (top) and scenes from the
Book of the Dead, including the Eye of Horus (above).

By centuries-old custom, they lived apart from other workers in a walled village of about 70 houses named the Place of Truth, now known as Deir el-Medina. It lay in the desert some distance from the valley, occupied by stonemasons, carpenters, sculptors, draftsmen, and painters—the elite of Egyptian craftspeople with skills that had been passed down for generations. An unusually literate community, they left copious records behind them, telling us how tomb workers were divided into two teams, a right and a left, who may have worked both sides of a sepulchre simultaneously under the supervision of a foreman. The actual hollowing out of the tomb with bronze-and-stone picks and mauls took a relatively short time. Even Seti's tomb may have taken no more than two years to excavate. Then the artisans moved in, working an eight-hour day, with a midday break and a day off every ten days, as well as special holidays during major festivals. Scribes were always present, keeping a log of attendance and monitoring progress.

The work was often harsh and demanding, taking a severe toll on young men's bodies. We know this, thanks to modern technology, which tells us more about some Egyptians' medical histories than they knew themselves. For example, Nakht was a Theban weaver who lived in about 1180 B.C. His mummy arrived at Canada's Royal Ontario Museum just under a century ago. He had received an elaborate burial for a weaver, but

Ramses II built his mortuary temple during a 20-year period, starting about

1277 B.C. Only parts of the pylons and the rear half of the inner temple still stand.

FOLLOWING PAGES: Seated figures of Ramses II greet visitors to the Great

Temple of Amun at Luxor. At left stands one of the obelisks erected by the king;

the other was removed to the Place de la Concorde in Paris during the 19th century.

x-rays showed his internal organs had not been removed, a procedure reserved for the wealthy. They also showed that he was a teenager who had suffered from prolonged malnutrition. Nakht's corpse, when unwrapped, proved to be remarkably whole. A two-day autopsy even recovered his complete brain, perfectly preserved in a waxy state. Nakht was 15 years old, stood 4 feet 8.25 inches tall, suffered from many chronic diseases but died of pneumonia. His lungs contained particles of red granite, which could have come only from granite quarries at Aswan far upstream from Thebes, a place of harsh punishment. Why he was sent to the quarries we do not, of course, know.

The task of decorating royal tombs took many years, which is why so many were never completed—with the exception of Seti's magnificent sepulchre. Betsy Bryan of Johns Hopkins University has studied the unfinished paintings in the tomb of Pharaoh Amenhotep II's royal butler Su-em-niwet, who served his master in the 15th century B.C. Su-em-niwet died early so his tomb paintings were never completed, giving Bryan an opportunity to study a commoner's tomb in progress. She found that a large team of artists of varying levels of competence worked in the tomb, laboring in different ways. Some of them specialized in certain types of composition, painters applying many layers of paint in different hues to achieve exactly the right color. Had the crudest paintings in the dark innermost chamber perhaps been executed by less-skilled artists and were awaiting completion by the master painters? No one knows for sure, but an anonymous master painter drew the figures in the well-lit front chamber in freehand, depicting the pharaoh and his queen with an assured, fine brush in perfect proportions and in subtle colors.

RAMSES THE GREAT

When Seti went to his ancestors, his 25-year-old son Ramses II ascended the throne and reigned for 66 years. He had been trained to be pharaoh from an early age, accompanying his father on expeditions against Egypt's enemies. "The Eldest King's Son" was constantly on the move, supervising the removal of obelisks from the quarries at Aswan, watching over his father's building projects, and assuming the trappings of high rank. An Abydos inscription states: "The All-Lord [Seti] himself made me great. . . . He equipped me with women, a royal harem as beautiful as that of the palace, those of the South and North were under my feet." The young Ramses also learned the military traditions cherished by his elders. Seti made

Ramses II expanded the Great Temple of Amun at Luxor and commemorated himself with statues at the same time. The two seated and four standing colossi of the king ennoble the entrance pylons, which are decorated with mighty deeds of battle.

sure his son would maintain the momentum of order and conquest he had begun.

The new pharaoh soon faced trouble in Asia. The Hittites had become dangerous adversaries in Syria, where Egypt competed with them for control of important trade routes. Seti had maintained control over the southern coastal ports, but the Hittites had taken possession of the strategic city of Kadesh on the Orontes River and pressed constantly against Egyptian interests. In year five of his reign (1274 B.C.), Ramses gathered together a huge army of 20,000 men divided into four regiments, named after Amun, Ptah, Re, and Seth. Like his illustrious predecessors he advanced rapidly across the Gaza Strip in spring and was only ten miles from Kadesh in early May.

Two captured spies claimed that the Hittite army was far to the north, so Ramses advanced with his Amun regiment. He crossed the Orontes and camped to the west of Kadesh, which had made itself into nearly an island by diverting water through canals. Fortunately for Ramses, one of his patrols captured two more spies. They admitted under torture that the previous spies had been planted to give false information. A huge Hittite army of about 37,000 men and 2,500 chariots under King Muwatallis was actually hiding out on the far side of Kadesh, ready to spring an ambush.

The Hittites descended in force on the Re regiment, which was advancing to join Ramses, scattered them in a few minutes, and attacked the royal camp. Ramses found himself alone except for his closest followers and his shield-bearer Menna. He rallied the survivors and was saved only by a unit of his relief force who came up in time to attack the Hittite flank. Under attack on two fronts King Muwatallis retreated as night fell. The next morning Ramses attacked with his entire army, but neither side prevailed after fierce fighting. Muwatallis proposed a truce, and the Egyptian army went home, leaving the situation exactly as it was before.

Ramses seized on the inconclusive Battle of Kadesh as an icon of his power. He told the story of his courage again and again on the walls of Karnak and Luxor, at temples at Abydos, el Derr, and Abu Simbel, deep in Nubia. His mortuary temple also told the familiar tale. Relief after relief shows the king towering over everyone, slaying the enemy, who scatter before him. The accompanying inscriptions recite his deeds in poetry and prose. They tell the story of the spies and Ramses' advance, of how he "took his seat on a throne of fine gold" near the Orontes where he learned of the nearby Hittite army "more numerous than the sands of the shores."

As the Hittite attack began, Ramses donned his armor "like Seth in the moment of his power," mounted his chariot "Victory-in-Thebes," and attacked his foes in fury.

"His majesty slew the entire force of the Foe from Khatti, together with his great chiefs and all his brothers . . . their infantry and their chariotry falling on their faces one upon the other...." After "the vile Chief of Khatti" suggested a truce, his majesty returned to Egypt. "He had crushed all lands through fear of him; his majesty's strength had protected his army, all foreign lands gave praise to his fair face."

The Egyptians mounted new campaigns against the Hittites in subsequent years, but Ramses eventually realized he could not hold northern Syria against his foes. By the same token the Hittite kings faced both internal unrest and a growing threat from the Assyrians. In 1259 B.C., 15 years after Kadesh, Ramses signed a formal peace treaty with King Hattusilis III, which took the form of a nonaggression pact. Thereafter the two civilizations enjoyed friendly relations, cemented by diplomatic marriages between Ramses and two of Hattusilis's daughters.

At home Egypt enjoyed a long period of prosperity. Ramses took eight principal wives, the chief among them being Nefertari, who died in about year 25 of his reign. He subsequently married Istnofret, who died a decade later. As was custom, Ramses took his later wives from his immediate family, including his younger sister and three of his own daughters, not to mention the two Hittite princesses. By the end of his long life, the pharaoh had sired 45 or more sons and uncounted numbers of daughters. Many of his sons predeceased him and were laid to rest in the now-famous KV 5 in the Valley of the Kings.

The ever energetic pharaoh embarked on an ambitious campaign of public works. Ramses was obsessed with power and with the intoxicating symbolism of architecture. He littered the country with huge statues of himself and is still omnipresent throughout Egypt. His architectural achievements were herculean—major additions at Karnak and Luxor, the completion of his father's shrine at Abydos, which he found neglected, and his own mortuary temple, the Ramesseum. At least 3,000 workers labored in the sandstone quarries at Gebel el-Silsila to cut stone for this temple alone.

In the delta the pharaoh founded his own capital city, a reflection of the growing importance of foreign affairs in Egypt's daily business. Pi-Ramses (Pi-Ramesse), "the house of Ramses, beloved of Amun, great of victories," lay close to ancient Avaris. The king's residence alone covered some four square miles, surrounded by temples, a military base, administrative buildings, and enormous gardens and orchards. Recently discovered military stables at the edge of the desert covered 18,300 square feet alone. Ramses traveled to his city regularly to attend religious festivals (Continued on page 242)

A grandiloquent propagandist, Ramses II never tired of boasting about his great battle with the Hittites at Kadesh in 1274 B.C. Although the outcome, in fact, had proved inconclusive, he commissioned reliefs of his "victory" on many temples, including the north wall of Karnak (below), Luxor, and the Ramesseum. The reliefs commemorate Ramses' bravery, aided by Amun—charging the enemy, smiting captives (left), and throwing the enemy into confusion.

NEFERTARI THE BEAUTIFUL

Queen Nefertari and Ramses II stand guard over the facade of her temple (left), a smaller version of his own temple a few hundred feet away at Abu Simbel. Smaller figures of their four children stand at their feet. Like Abu Simbel itself, this carved cliff face resembles the sloping walls of a temple pylon with 33-foot-high statues cut into niches in the rock. "Possessor of charm, sweetness, and love," Nefertari was probably the daughter of a prominent official, Bakenkhons. She disappeared from history soon after the dedication of her temple and died in about 1254 B.C. The great queen was buried in splendor in Ta Set Neferu, the Valley of the Queens, on the west bank of the Nile close to the pharaohs' desolate resting place. Her rock-cut tomb, famous for its stucco relief paintings (recently restored by the Getty Conservation Institute), shows the graceful Nefertari herself, wearing all her finery, making offerings to the major deities (above).

RAMSES: EPITOME OF EGYPT'S POWER

Ramses II, "the Great," epitomized Egypt at the height of its power. Born about 1304 B.C., he ruled for 66 years, living into his 90s. His architects chose a poor spot for his tomb where the rock was soft. Wall collapses and floods have ruined the deep sepulchre and destroyed many of the superb wall paintings. Constellations and deities once adorned the burial chamber, while the antechamber bore scenes from the *Book of the Dead*. Ramses did not lie in his tomb long. Necropolis priests snatched his mummy away in the face of looters. Eventually it came to rest in a deep rock cleft with other royal mummies. Ramses remained undisturbed until 1881 when tomb robbers discovered the hiding place. Fortunately recovered by archaeologists and stabilized by French conservators in 1976, Ramses now lies in the Cairo Museum (left). He was a king of imposing profile, with strong jaw and nose. Medical technology reveals that Ramses suffered from arthritis, dental abscesses, and poor circulation.

and to escape the summer heat upstream. Little remains of Pi-Ramses today, but it may have been the city where the Hebrews labored in "the land of Goshen." Pi-Ramses may also have been the city from which the Israelite exodus began; no reference to the Biblical diaspora has been found in Egyptian records.

The most famous of all Ramses' buildings lies far upstream—the two great temples overlooking the Nile at Abu Simbel in Lower Nubia. Ramses built seven rock-cut temples above the First Cataract, but the most ambitious was Abu Simbel. He boasted how "multitudes of workmen from the captivity of his sword in every land" labored on Abu Simbel. His prisoners started work in about the fifth year of his reign and labored for nearly 20 years until 1256 B.C.

Four huge seated statues of Ramses, each about 66 feet high, form the facade of the Great Temple. The king gazes serenely into the distance, wearing the double crown of Egypt and the royal nemes headdress. Bound African and Asiatic captives lie beneath the statues, to the south and north respectively. His mother and Queen Nefertari, as well as several children, stand at his feet.

Entry into the temple takes one under a figure of Re flanked by images of the king. The god carries the symbols of power and truth, forming a rebus of Ramses'

Ramses II fathered scores of sons, many of them possibly buried in tomb KV 5.

The eastern wall of the hypostyle hall shows the king and his sons attacking a Hittite

fortress; the pharaoh stands before the god Osiris as his sons parade below him.

FOLLOWING PAGES: Egyptologists Kent and Susan Weeks examine reliefs

of Hathor and Osiris on the wall of Tomb KV 5 in the Valley of the Kings.

throne name (User-Maat-Re: "the justice of Re is strong"). Inside, battle scenes, including the ubiquitous Battle of Kadesh, adorn a pillared hall decorated with large statues of the king as Osiris. The inner sanctuary contains a small altar and, in a rear niche, seated statues of Amun-Re, Ptah, the deified Ramses, and Re-Horakhty. A smaller temple in honor of Nefertari and the goddess Hathor lies immediately to the south, adorned with four 35-foot statues of Ramses and two of his queens.

Abu Simbel faces eastward toward the rising sun. Each morning the first brilliant rays illuminate a row of carved baboons atop the facade, always the symbolic greeters of the sun god. Next the climbing sun lights up the royal statues and the image of Amun-Re over the entrance, then enters the temple itself. Twice a year, on October 22 and February 22, the sun's rays penetrate some 200 feet into the sanctuary where they illuminate all the statues in the rear sanctuary except the creator, Ptah.

Why did the pharaoh spend so lavishly on Abu Simbel? The answer lies in one word—gold. Ramses needed enormous quantities of gold to support new construction and to conduct foreign affairs. A peaceful, well organized Nubia provided much of it.

The pharaohs had long memories and never forgot how the Kingdom of Kush had taken advantage of a divided Egypt. They adopted draconian measures to prevent a repeat. Ahmose had begun the process of conquest at the beginning of the New Kingdom, but it was Thutmose I who sacked Kerma and established indirect rule over Upper Nubia through vassal chieftains. The objective was simple: Control the lucrative trade that flowed down the river. Late in the reign of Thutmose II (ca 1480 B.C.), gold production from Nubia had reached a staggering 572 pounds annually. The figure rose even higher in later centuries. Rebellious Nubian chieftains resented paying tribute to distant masters. Periodically an Egyptian army would descend, execute some rebels, and take hundreds of prisoners. Within a few generations unrest erupted yet again. By this time the pharaohs could endure the repeated provocation no more. Thutmose I marched south and occupied the densely populated Dongola Reach region far upstream. Thereafter Nubia became an Egyptian colony. Military activity was confined to campaigns against raiding desert groups.

The New Kingdom pharaohs adopted different imperial policies in Asia and Nubia. In Asia they insisted that the rulers of small states acknowledge their overlordship and pay tribute. They established strategic garrisons under Egyptian military control to maintain the pharaoh's interests. At the same time they left the social and political structures of subject kingdoms intact, partly because the Egyptians respected and

Nut, goddess of the sky, lies outstretched inside the sarcophagus of Ramses II's

son, Pharaoh Merneptah. Kha-bewes, a name for Nut that means "the one

with a thousand souls," extended herself over the sky, the constellations forming

her clothing. She protected the dead king, who rose into her heavenly abode.

needed Levantine skills in weaving, metalworking, and other crafts, and also because they admired their ancient religious beliefs. The Nubians received no such respect. The pharaohs simply reorganized Lower Nubia along Egyptian lines into a vassal state that existed to supply gold, other material goods, and slaves.

The king appointed a senior official as "King's Son of Kush" with responsibility for administering Nubia and ensuring its taxes were paid on time. A hierarchical bureaucracy modeled on Egyptian lines administered Lower Nubia, complete with the usual army of scribes and a strong military presence. Egyptian colonists settled throughout the colony to take key administrative positions. The Nubian chiefs living farther upstream along the strategic Dongola Reach were allowed a considerable amount of autonomy under the watchful eye of a few Egyptian officials. In this way the Egyptians co-opted local leaders who had once owed allegiance to the quite sophisticated Kerma state. Large towns and numerous temples were founded, among them a large temple to Amun at Jebel Barkal, which the local people regarded as the Throne of Amun. Local chiefs retained nominal sovereignty over their lands. Their sons traveled as hostages to the Egyptian court to be schooled alongside the princes of Asiatic rulers, where "they heard the speech of the Egyptians in the retinue of their king" and forgot their own language.

A new Lower Nubian nobility arose over the centuries, with closer ties and loyalties to their opposite numbers in Egypt than to their own people. Inscriptions show returning princes living like wealthy Egyptians—inspecting their plantations, hunting from chariots, and enjoying the good life. The tomb of the vizier Huy at Thebes shows Lower Nubian nobility in a delegation to the court wearing fashionable Egyptian clothing, indistinguishable from royal courtiers except for their feather headdresses, black skins, and elaborate sashes. Meanwhile most Nubians worked as humble laborers on land owned by the pharaoh, temple priests, or local nobility and administrators. For almost five centuries Nubia was subjected to an intensive program of Egyptianization in the name of gold. The colony's gold mines were closely supervised at every turn, worked by slaves, prisoners of war, and convicts laboring under extremely harsh conditions. So forbidding was gold mine service that it became part of a legal oath: "If I lie, may my nose and ears be cut off and I be sent to Kush."

Ramses II ruled over a kingdom whose wealth was fabled throughout the eastern Mediterranean world. When he died in his nineties about 1213 B.C., he left behind an Egypt at the height of its powers.

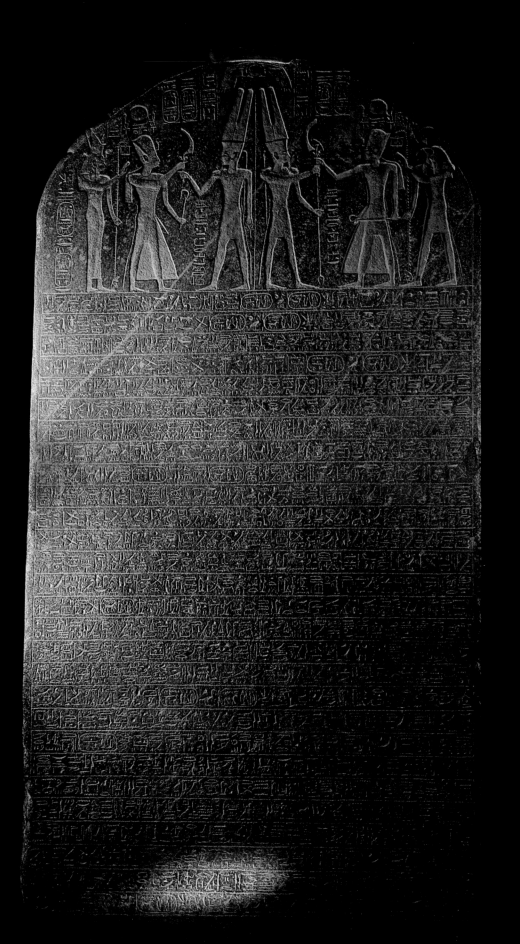

This stela commemorates the victory of Pharaoh Merneptah, Ramses II's 13th son, who suppressed a revolt in Asia and "destroyed the seeds of the Israeli people."

FOLLOWING PAGES: The goddess Nut encircles the heavens on the ceiling of Ramses VI's burial chamber; the sun is swallowed in the body of the goddess, then reborn. The sun god then sails across the heavens in the solar bark.

PALACE PLOTS AND SEA PEOPLES

Ramses died as stability on Egypt's frontiers deteriorated. The Hittites had become good allies, but were now under pressure along their northern frontiers. Drought and crop failure threatened their well-being. His 13th son Merneptah reigned for about ten years during which he suppressed revolts in Libya and Nubia. Boasts his inscription at Karnak: "Libyans, slain, whose uncircumcised phalli were carried off 6,259." When the Hittites invoked their treaty of mutual support with Egypt, the king sent cargoes of grain north to alleviate hunger.

Confusion reigned after Merneptah's death around 1204 until Ramses III of the 20th dynasty came to the throne about 1187. He was the last of the great pharaohs but ruled at a time of intensifying difficulties beyond his frontiers. His first challenge was a Libyan incursion into the delta, which the pharaoh's army repelled with great slaughter. The survivors were enslaved. Such infiltrations were routine in times of drought when desert peoples cast covetous eyes on the fertile valley. Libyan troubles paled into insignificance alongside the tumultuous events unfolding in Asia, which brought the Sea Peoples to the gates of Egypt.

Sea Peoples—the name conjures up bold mercantile adventurers, perhaps comparable to the Vikings of a later time and place. In fact the hordes of Sea Peoples had no specific ethnic or national identity. Many were seafarers and merchants from Aegean and eastern Mediterranean ports who spent their lives on the move from harbor to harbor from Italy to the Nile. Some of the Sea Peoples were desert nomads, cattle herders, or farmers. At best they were a loosely knit confederation of coastal groups, including the Philistines of the Levant and others from as far afield as the Aegean and Sicily. In a cosmopolitan world they were the wanderers, the seamen, and the professional warriors, living from hand to mouth, and particularly vulnerable to drought and famine. In about 1200 B.C., widespread crop failures wreaked havoc in the Hittite Empire. The desperate Sea Peoples turned against the Hittites and overthrew them. Then they attacked Egypt from Syria, a horde on the move, complete with oxcarts, women, and children, who planned not just to raid the Nile Valley but also to settle there.

Hundreds of ships sailed alongside attackers on land. Ramses manned his borders and slaughtered the invaders with himself at the army's front—as he tells us in a long inscription on his mortuary temple at Medinet Habu, "the Mansion of Millions of Years of King Ramses III, United with Eternity in the Estate of Amun."

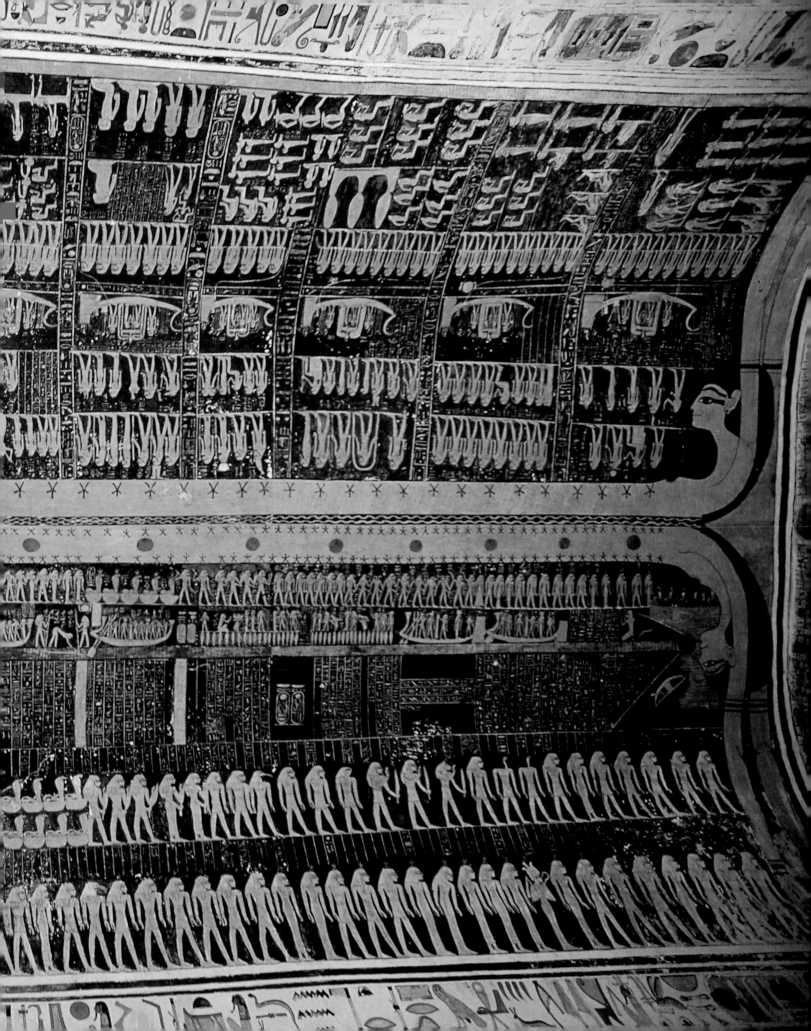

The enemy fleet now approached an eastern mouth of the Nile, where the Egyptian navy confronted them. Archers lined the banks and bulwarks of Egyptian warships, pouring volleys of arrows into the attackers' ships as soon as they were in range. The reliefs at Medinet Habu show the archers calmly mowing down the foe as grappling irons brought the enemy vessels close alongside.

The Sea People were annihilated and the threat of invasion receded, only to be followed by another attack, this time from the west, when Libyans once again tried to infiltrate the delta.

Again Ramses prevailed, killing more than 2,000 attackers and capturing vast numbers of cattle. A fascinating relief on the north wall of Medinet Habu recounts how military scribes bring a tally of enemy dead before the king: 175 severed right hands are piled before him. The king questions the numbers, until the scribes dutifully assemble the dead's 175 severed penises—and the numbers coincide.

As the king reached the end of his 31-year reign, the palace seethed with intrigue over the succession. One of Ramses' minor queens, Tiye, plotted to assassinate the king so that her son Pentewere could seize the throne. The plotters even planned to use forbidden spells from a stolen book of royal magic to paralyze key guards. The

Pharaoh Amenhotep II's tomb served as a refuge for at least nine other kings, to save them from looters. Necropolis priests stashed the bodies into two sealed chambers here. Roll call included Amenhotep III, Merneptah, and Thutmose IV.

foiled plot reached deep into the royal harem. A judicial papyrus in the Turin Museum tells us how Ramses appointed 14 officials to sit in judgment on the 40 accused, including 4 royal butlers. He gave the panel full authority to collect evidence, deliver a verdict, even execute those convicted.

The prisoners were tried in groups: 28 people, including the ringleaders and Queen Tiye, were condemned and presumably sentenced to death; 6 others were forced to commit suicide in court; 4 others, including Prince Pentewere, were permitted to do so in their cells. The final group of accused included 3 judges and 2 officers appointed to the case, who were accused of entertaining several women conspirators and others of the prisoners. Of the 5, 4 were found guilty and sentenced to have their ears and noses amputated; one of them committed suicide. The pharaoh may have died before the verdicts were reached. With him ended Egypt's greatest era. His successors reigned for merely a few years. When Ramses VI came to the throne in 1145 B.C., the country was roiling with unrest.

Egypt's eastern frontier was under attack. The frontier shrank from the Levant to the edge of the eastern delta. The state even abandoned the turquoise mines of Sinai. Prices climbed rapidly at home as supplies of gold from Nubia dried up and the mines in the Wadi el-Allaqi system ceased to be productive. The pharaoh now lacked the labor and resources to work the mines on a large enough scale. At home even the building of royal tombs was in trouble. The necropolis workers at Deir el-Medina went on strike when they were not paid for six months.

The political center of gravity moved northward into the delta, leaving Thebes and its environs in the hands of the ever powerful priesthood of Amun, which was so rich with the land and wealth showered on it by generations of pharaohs that it was nearly the most potent economic force in the land.

By time of Ramses XI (1104-1075 B.C.), Egypt was once again effectively two countries, with the pharaoh ruling in the north and the high priest of Amun at Thebes in control of Upper Egypt. The fabled wealth of the country had ebbed, in part because there was more gold below ground with the dead than in the domain of the living. Egypt's renowned diplomatic clout faded with her wealth. The pharaoh's officials feared to travel abroad and often were robbed.

Ramses XI was never buried in the Valley of the Kings. His abandoned tomb became a workshop, where the necropolis priests stripped royal coffins and mummies of their gold and other valuables before they were moved to new locations.

THE LATE PERIOD

The Temple of Kalabsha (ancient Talmis) stands above the waters of man-made Lake Nasser. The last of the Ptolemies and the Roman Emperor Augustus built Kalabsha in honor of the Nubian god Horus-Mandulis, also Isis and Osiris. Later the temple sanctuary served as a Christian church. Like Abu Simbel, Kalabsha was moved to higher ground when threatened by the building of the Aswan High Dam.

THE LATE PERIOD

This gilded mummy from the Valley of the Mummies at Bahariya Oasis southeast of Cairo exemplifies the wealth of Greco-Roman Egypt long after the great pharaohs had been forgotten. During the post-pharaonic era Egypt's fabled wealth slowly evaporated. Nubian kings took over the country, but the Assyrians prevailed in 663 B.C., when King Ashurbanipal sacked Thebes. Later Egypt regained her independence, and after 653 B.C. Saite kings governed the country like merchant kings. The Persians arrived in 525 B.C., followed by Alexander the Great in 332. After his death the Ptolemies established a Greek dynasty that endured nearly 300 years and turned Egypt into an economic powerhouse. Traditionalists resented Greek influence and clung to the old ways. In 30 B.C. Egypt became a Roman province.

Second Intermediate	New Kingdom	Third Intermediate Period	Late Period	Greco-Roman Age
ca 1630–1520 B.C.	ca 1539–1070 B.C.	ca 1075–715 B.C.	ca 715–332 B.C.	332 B.C.–A.D. 395

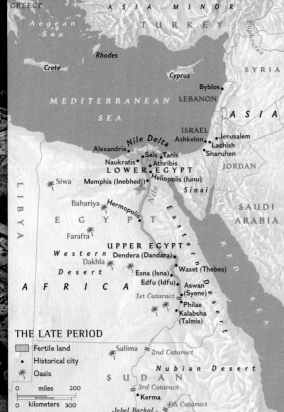

THE LATE PERIOD

- Fertile land
- Historical city
- Oasis

0 — miles — 200
0 — kilometers — 300

Historical drainage and coastlines are represented on this map; country boundaries are current.

Dynasty 21 (Tanis)

Smendes I
Amenemnisu
Psusennes I
Amenemope
Osorkon I
Siamun
Psusennes II

(Thebes—High Priests)

Herihor
Piankh
Pinedjem I
Masaherta
Menkheperre
Smendes II
Pinedjem II

Psusennes III

Dynasty 22
LIBYAN

Shoshenq I
Osorkon II
Takelot I
Shoshenq II
Osorkon III
Takelot II
Shoshenq III
Pami
Shoshenq V
Osorkon V
Harsiese (Thebes)

Dynasty 23
LIBYAN

Pedibastet
Shoshenq IV
Osorkon IV
Takelot III
Rudamon
Iuput
Nimlot
Peftjauawybast

Dynasty 24

Tefnakhte
Bakenrenef

Dynasty 25
NUBIAN

Kashta
Piye

NUBIAN

Shabaka
Shebitku
Taharqa
Tantamani

Dynasty 26

Psamtek I
Necho II
Psamtek II
Apries
Amasis
Psamtek III

Dynasty 27
PERSIAN

Cambyses
Darius I
Xerxes
Artaxerxes I
Darius II

Dynasty 28
(Persians expelled)

Amyrtaeus

Dynasty 29

Nepherites I
Psammuthis
Hakor
Nepherites II

Dynasty 30

Nectanebo I
Djedhor
Nectanebo II

Dynasty 31
PERSIAN

Artaxerxes III
Arses
Darius III

Macedonian Dynasty
Alexander the Great

Ptolemaic Dynasty
Cleopatra VII

Roman Emperors

SCANDAL AT THEBES

We can imagine the careful plotting beforehand, the secret rendezvous in a desolate ravine, quiet figures moving stealthily through the pitch-black Egyptian night. Frantic digging in the dark, oil lamps in hand, the robbers grab as much portable treasure as they can and slip away before the sun rises. The robbery was unavoidable. Every Egyptian knew the rich and powerful took treasure with them to eternity. Even one ornament from a pharaoh's sepulchre could keep a poor villager in food for years. Tomb robbing became epidemic as Egypt fell on troubled times. During the 16th year of Ramses IX (ca 1110 B.C.), a major scandal erupted in Thebes where rumors of surreptitious digging had circulated for years. The case involved Paser, the mayor of Thebes, an honest local bureaucrat. Paser started an official investigation into tomb robbing and soon uncovered testimony

A mythic stand of reeds in stone (opposite), the columns of the hypostyle hall at the temple of Horus (above) at Edfu, in Upper Egypt, present an illusion of the shadowy primordial swamp of creation. Finished by the Ptolemies between 237 and 57 B.C., Edfu is the most completely preserved of ancient Egyptian temples.

The silver sarcophagus of Pharaoh Psusennes I (ca 1040-995 B.C.) was discovered by French Egyptologist Pierre Montet in 1939. Ancient Egyptians considered silver to be the bones of the gods and gold to be their flesh. Psusennes wears the formal regalia of kingship and carries the pharaoh's crook and flail.

from eyewitnesses. Paser laid his case before the local vizier, who sent an official commission to inspect the tombs. A quick cover-up on the west bank ensured they found little out of order.

Paser was a determined man. He continued to bombard the vizier with evidence of tomb robbing. A year later even the highest officials could not deny that something was wrong. The vizier convened a new inquiry. Forty-five tomb robbers were brought before the court and beaten on the soles of their feet to extract confessions. Their testimony survives, ironically on papyri looted and sold to 19th-century tourists. The case ended with savage punishments for the offenders, which probably included death by impalement. Some of the accused were acquitted when it became obvious that beatings produced false testimony. Not that the cases did much to stem the flood of robberies, for there are isolated mentions of later trials.

A LAND IN TROUBLE

A thousand years before Christ, the great pharaohs were but a memory. The Egyptians had been zestful conquerors during the 18th dynasty, but after the Akhenaten debacle their armies were largely made up of foreign mercenaries from Libya, Nubia, and eastern Mediterranean lands. Egypt lost some of its self-confidence and turned in on itself. The people lived under a comfortable bureaucracy with opportunities to obtain quiet hereditary offices. The priesthood of Amun acquired more wealth and a great deal more political and economic influence.

The military effectively took over the Theban priesthood in about 1085 B.C. Herihor, a general who had served as viceroy of Kush and vizier, became high priest. He was powerful enough to assert his authority over the last of the Ramessids and to establish his own ruling class with Ramses XI's sister Nodjmet as his wife. He ruled for six years alongside the pharaoh but predeceased him. By this time the center of political power was in the north where 19th and 20th dynasty kings, such as Ramses II, had founded important ports on the Mediterranean. These cosmopolitan cities and their thriving markets reflected Egypt's increasing involvement in the swirling crosscurrents of eastern Mediterranean politics.

The dual rulership continued after Ramses XI's death with the rulers of Thebes paying at least nominal homage to the king at Tanis, a city in the northeastern delta. Seven 21st dynasty kings ruled from Tanis between 1075 and 945 B.C. The pharaohs

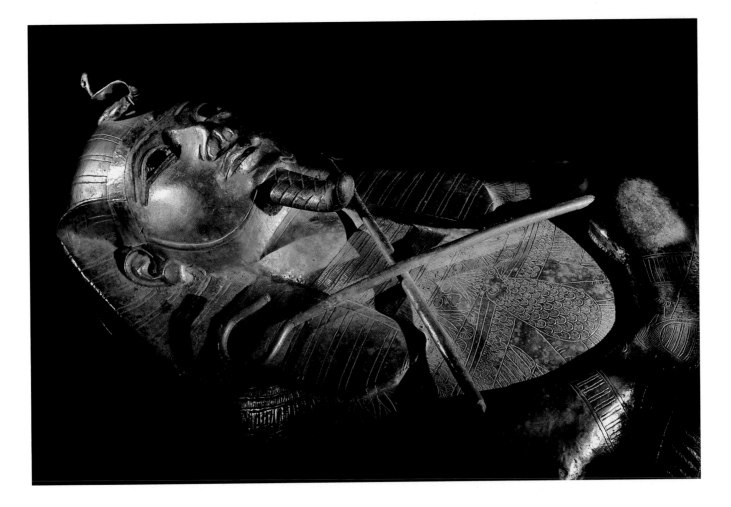

were much preoccupied with political events in Asia as David tried to unite the Israelites and destroy the Philistines. For centuries Asian princesses had made diplomatic marriages with the Egyptian court. Now the no-longer-so-proud pharaohs sent Egyptian princesses to such luminaries as Hadad, the crown prince of Edom. An Egyptian princess also married King Solomon of Israel. The pharaoh's armies still campaigned in Asia, capturing Gezer from the Philistines, an event mentioned in the Bible.

In 1939-40 French Egyptologist Pierre Montet found the burial chambers of the 21st dynasty kings below the pavement of a temple to the gods Amun, Mut, and Khonsu at Tanis. The rich tomb of King Psusennes (ca 1040-995 B.C.) was intact, the only completely undisturbed royal sepulchre ever found in Egypt. (Tutankhamun's was disturbed twice soon after sealing.) The king wore a golden mask somewhat like that of Tutankhamun but of lesser workmanship. Little of the mummy survived inside the silver inner coffin, which lay, in turn, in a black granite anthropoid coffin that had once belonged to a 19th dynasty noble. The coffins sat inside a red granite sarcophagus used more than 200 years earlier for the burial of King Merneptah, the successor of Ramses II. Such recycling would have been unheard of in earlier times and may be a sign that the tombs in the Valley of the Kings were being looted.

In about 945 B.C. royal power passed to a series of Libyan chiefs, who ruled during the 22nd and 23rd dynasties. The founder, Shoshenq I, former commander-in-chief of armed forces, was a strong ruler who reunited Tanis and Thebes. Shoshenq maintained power by placing members of his family in key posts throughout the country. He reasserted the Egyptian presence in Asia with a campaign against the kingdoms of Judah and Israel in 925 B.C. The pharaoh surrounded Jerusalem but was bought off by "the treasures of the house of the Lord, and the treasures of the king's house; he even took away all: and he took away all the shields of gold which Solomon had made."

His triumph was short-lived. Serious trouble soon loomed in the east. Casting covetous eyes on the rich markets and cities of the Levant, the Assyrian Kings Ashurnasirpal II and his son Shalmaneser III (ca 858-828 B.C) campaigned in Syria and Palestine. In 853 B.C. Egypt entered into an alliance with Israel and Byblos. Together they halted the Assyrian advance, but Egypt was in trouble at home, despite the 50-year reign of King Shoshenq III (ca 835-785 B.C). The south split from the north, and the delta separated into kingdoms dominated by different cities. With the death of King Shoshenq III a series of minor kings presided over Lower Egypt and quarreled amongst themselves as the country went into economic and political decline.

Egypt's fabulous wealth in gold slowly evaporated although the memory lingered. "Egyptian Thebes where the houses overflow with the greatest troves of treasure, Thebes with the hundred gates," wrote Homer in the *Iliad*, set down about 750 B.C. There were still many wealthy Egyptian families, but they were plagued with the same kinds of health problems as their more lowly countrymen. For example in about 850 B.C., a woman named Djedmaatesankh, a chantress at the Great Temple of Amun at Karnak in Thebes, was buried in a beautifully rendered coffin after mummification. Her untouched mummy came to Toronto's Royal Ontario Museum in 1910 and had never been studied until modern medical technology allowed its examination without opening the coffin. She received a complete body CT scan in 1977 and another one with much more sophisticated technology in 1994. Djed had died in agony, the result of a massive abscess in her upper jaw, a common condition in ancient Egyptians.

Without gold the pharaohs lost their diplomatic clout and the means to power in Asia. Egypt ceased to be the land of ease and wealth in foreign eyes that it had been for centuries—the Shangri-la of the ancient world, as Egyptologist Peter Clayton calls it. Its rulers were no longer awesome god-kings who maintained a world of order in the face of chaos. They were merely commonplace monarchs, struggling to survive in an ever more complex world. Egypt was a state in name only, with a constant ebb and flow of breakaway kingdoms, especially in the delta. But about 730 B.C. the various local rulers came together against a new threat, this time from the south. Nubia was expanding into the territory of its former master.

NUBIAN PHARAOHS

Nubia had gone its own way since the days of Ramses XI when the viceroy of Kush, perhaps of Nubian birth, had attempted a coup against the throne, had been defeated by Herihor, and had fled far south into Nubia. An important new kingdom of Kush developed in the Napata region, downstream of the Fourth Cataract in Upper Nubia and close to the great shrine of Amun at Jebel Barkal. The Napatan kings traded with Egypt and kept a firm pulse on changing political events upstream but retained their own African culture.

Eighth-century Napatan King Kashta, the sixth of his line, journeyed north to Thebes. A recent convert to the worship of Amun, Kashta portrayed himself as a pilgrim, a defender of the true faith, perhaps in an attempt to legitimize Kushite and Theban ambitions to take over all of Egypt. Amun's priests sanctified his royal line and a formal alliance between Napata and Thebes. Centuries of enmity between African and Egyptian gave way to a remarkably equal partnership.

Kashta died in about 750 B.C. His son Piye spent the first 20 years of his reign at Napata. But word reached him of threats against Thebes by a delta leader named Tefnakht, who wanted to bring all Egypt under his rule. Military officials at Thebes implored Piye to protect the domains of Amun against the invader. The details of what followed come to us from a commemorative stela erected by Piye at Jebel Barkal.

Urging the Thebans to resist as best they could, the king sent an army north. His generals drove Tefnakht away but did not destroy his forces. The king now arrived in person to finish off the job. With brilliant political opportunism Piye participated in the Opet festival at Thebes, causing the statue of Amun to be paraded along the traditional processional way, just as it had been in the days of the great pharaohs. This gesture appealed to the traditionalists and brought him the support of Upper Egypt.

In about 730 B.C. Piye moved against an uneasy coalition of four kings to the north. He defeated them easily but treated them leniently, more as individuals who had made stupid mistakes than as rebels. Next he turned against troublemakers

farther downstream. He besieged Hermopolis in Middle Egypt where the ruler Nim-lot surrendered all his treasure, including his own crown, and sent his wife out to plead for his life. The austere Piye inspected the palace and treasury, then headed for the "stables of his horses and the quarters of the foals. When he saw that they had suffered hunger, he said: 'I swear as Re loves me...it is more grievous...that my horses have suf-fered hunger than any evil deed that thou hast done....'"

Piye returned to Thebes, adopted the coronation names of Thutmose III and Ram-ses II, and then, inexplicably, returned to his Nubian home. He never visited Egypt again. Inevitably the rebels he had treated leniently and refused to deal with because "they were uncircumcised and eaters of flesh" merely resumed their power struggles.

Piye's brother Shabaka managed to establish control over all of Egypt after 715 B.C. He was as zealous as his sibling in reviving ancient religious beliefs and customs. Shabaka embarked on major building works at Thebes, Dendera, Esna, and other tem-ples, all to the glory of Amun and other Egyptian gods, but one of his main preoccupations was the increasingly aggressive Assyrians. He managed to keep King Sargon II at bay, but his successors were less successful. Sargon had been preoccupied with troubles elsewhere in his empire, but King Sennacherib descended on rebellious

The Nubian Pharaoh Taharqa ascended the throne of Egypt about 690 B.C.
A devout traditionalist, he worked hard to restore the Temple of Amun at Karnak
and undertook other ambitious building works. But after the defeat of his armies
by the Assyrians, Taharqa fled south, deep into Nubia.

Israel in force, laid siege to the city of Lachish (an event mentioned in the Bible's Second Book of Kings), and forced the Judaean King Hezekiah to surrender Jerusalem. Pharaoh Shebitku had allied himself with the rebels but had done little to help them. Sennacherib contemptuously dismissed the once powerful Egypt as a broken reed: "Now behold, thou trustest upon the staff of this broken reed, even upon Egypt, whereon, if a man leans, it will go into his hand and pierce it; so is Pharaoh, king of Egypt, unto all that trust on him."

Another Nubian named Taharqa became pharaoh about 690 B.C. and enjoyed a brief respite from Assyrian ambitions, although the country was far from united under his rule. He was an able man but reaped the whirlwind of his predecessor's ambitions in Asia. After Assyrian King Sennacherib was assassinated in Nineveh around 681 B.C., an alliance between Taharqa's army and the city of Ashkelon drove back the armies of King Sennacherib's son Esarhaddon about 674 B.C. In the intervals between his Asian campaigns Taharqa invested heavily in buildings for Amun, which commemorated the ancient religious order. A vengeful Esarhaddon struck deep into Egypt circa 671 B.C. and captured Memphis and most of the royal family except Taharqa, who fled south.

The defiant Egyptians rebelled again and again, notably under the pharaoh Tantamani, Taharqa's cousin. Emboldened by visions of ancient greatness, Tantamani swept northward through Egypt and recaptured Memphis. His fortune was short-lived. An enraged King Ashurbanipal descended on the Nile with a large army in 667 B.C., repossessed Memphis, and sacked Thebes in a vicious attack that sent shock waves through the eastern Mediterranean world. Karnak and Luxor were ransacked, the royal treasuries emptied, the ancient holy city devastated. Tantamani fled southward to Napata and never returned as the Assyrians consolidated their hold on the land south of Aswan. The century-long Nubian dynasty ended with his death about 657 B.C.

SAITES AND PERSIANS

As was their custom, the Assyrians appointed a puppet ruler over their new and divided domains. In 665 B.C. Ashurbanipal had made a local noble named Necho, king of the delta city of Sais and his son Psamtek (also known as Psammetichus) ruler of Athribis, also in the delta. Necho died the following year, so it fell to Psamtek to reconcile Lower Egypt with Thebes. He was fortunate in receiving the support of Mentuemhet, prince and mayor of Thebes, *(Continued on page 270)*

IUFAA'S TOMB

In 1998 Czech Egyptologists discovered the sepulchre
of a hitherto unknown 27th dynasty priest named
Iufaa at the sacred 5th dynasty pyramid complex of
Abusir. Iufaa served Pharaohs Amasis and Psamtek III
and was buried during the Persian occupation of
Darius I (521 B.C.). His sepulchre boasted a mud-brick
enclosure wall, a deep main shaft, and a burial chamber
still sealed off with the original boulders, whose walls
bore beautifully preserved inscriptions and reliefs.
The Czechs Ladislav Bareš and Miroslav Verner opened
Iufaa's undisturbed massive stone sarcophagus in 1998
(left), lifting the lid with infinite care and revealing
a basalt anthropoid sarcophagus (above), which held
the mummy, badly damaged by moisture from the
high water table. Iufaa went to the afterlife accompanied by numerous non-Egyptian clay vessels and
no less than 408 faience *shabti* figures to serve him
throughout eternity.

The mummy of the priest Iufaa wore a superb covering of faience beads (opposite). The protective goddess Isis spreads her wings on Iufaa's chest. Before moisture did its damage, his head had been gilded. Once removed from its sarcophagus, the mummy was packed carefully in a specially constructed plywood case. In a modern funerary procession, workers carried Iufaa to a waiting vehicle; the Abusir pyramids loom in the distance (below). Then the mummy went to a laboratory in Giza, near Cairo. Originally the excavators assumed Iufaa was an old man, but medical technology proved them wrong. After anthropologists unwrapped the mummy and recovered the amulets bandaged with it, x-rays probed Iufaa's desiccated corpse (see skull, right) and established his age at between 25 and 35.

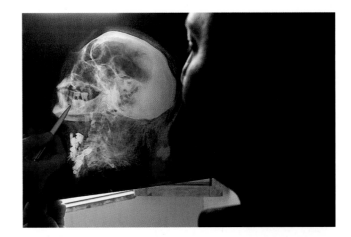

who was powerful among the surviving Theban nobility and a former right-hand man of Taharqa. Psamtek recruited a large mercenary army, including many Greeks, to subdue his delta rivals.

Fortunately for Egypt Psamtek reigned for more than half a century, bringing much needed stability to a country where the prestige of the pharaoh was severely diminished. He and his Saite successors governed more as merchant princes than as divine rulers in a world that saw Assyria's power decline rapidly. In 653 B.C. Psamtek boldly cast off the foreign yoke while the Assyrians were preoccupied with their own internal problems. By the time the Assyrian capital at Nineveh was sacked by the Persians and Scythians about 612 B.C., Egypt was once again a prosperous independent state but in a vastly changed world where international trade was as important as autonomy.

Rebellion against the Saites seethed below the surface among traditionalists, who hankered for simpler days. Fierce resentment against foreigners led to mutinies and uprisings at home. Around 570 civil war between mercenaries and local Egyptian soldiers ended in a pitched battle, won by the indigenous army under General Amasis, who promptly became pharaoh. He sought to reduce ethnic tensions by granting special trading privileges to foreigners who settled at the city of Naukratis, in the delta, making it an ancient equivalent of a free-trade zone. A cornerstone of his policy was to reach out to other states and potential markets.

While Amasis encouraged foreign trade, the Persians cast their covetous eyes on Egypt. Only a year after Psamtek III came to the throne about 526 B.C., he had to face an invasion in force by King Cambyses. The inexperienced pharaoh's army was no match for well-equipped and experienced Persian regiments, who used Bedouin guides to cross the desert swiftly. The Egyptians were routed, and Psamtek III fled to Memphis where he was captured and sent into exile.

Herodotus, who visited Egypt three quarters of a century later, wrote about the outrageous acts of King Cambyses. For example when he heard rejoicing the day after Memphis fell and learned that the people were celebrating the birth of a new sacred Apis bull, he ordered it brought into his presence and speared it with his own hand—an outrageous and unholy act in light of the bull's meaning: The cult of the sacred bull went back to the Old Kingdom, perhaps even earlier. The living Apis bull was the manifestation of the god Ptah, creator god of Memphis. Every Apis bull had the same coloring: black with a white diamond mark on the forehead and other distinctive characteristics. A special team of priests tended the bull, who lived in pampered luxury in

Ptah's temple at Memphis. Apis was an oracle and prophet, a source of wisdom, with attendants who observed and interpreted his every move. When Apis died, the country went into mourning. The discovery of a new Apis bull with the correct colorings was an occasion for great rejoicing.

Cambyses also desecrated Amasis's mummy and caused it to be burned, symbolically depriving the dead king of immortality. After his initial successes Cambyses fared badly. He is said to have lost an entire army in the desert while searching for Siwa Oasis. Reports of finding the "lost army" still surface occasionally in the popular press.

Darius I succeeded Cambyses in 521 and took a much closer interest in the administration of Egypt. But Darius was distracted by events elsewhere, especially his war against the Greeks, which ended with his defeat at the Battle of Marathon in 490 B.C. The Egyptians took advantage of the situation and rebelled against Persian rule. King Xerxes retaliated savagely, leaving his cruel son Achaemenes to rule as satrap. Xerxes was assassinated in 466. The Egyptians rebelled yet again under the leadership of Princes Inaros of Heliopolis and Amyrtaeus of Sais. At first they were victorious with the help of Greek allies, but the Persians soon prevailed and Inaros was executed.

New revolts broke out in the time of King Darius II (424-404 B.C.), with so much success that Egypt enjoyed quasi-independence during the rule of Darius II and Artaxerxes I, the last two Persian monarchs of the 27th dynasty. The final Persian advance against Egypt came in 343 B.C., when Pharaoh Nectanebo II faced an attack at Pelusium with an army that included more than 20,000 Greek mercenaries. A Greek general on the Persian side outflanked the Egyptians, captured Pelusium and other delta cities, then Memphis. Pharaoh Nectanebo fled southward to Nubia, and the reign of the last native Egyptian pharaoh ended. According to later Greek accounts the Persians continued to administer Egypt harshly, robbing temple treasuries, slaughtering sacred animals, and demanding taxes. But this time the Persian occupation lasted but a decade. The last Persian satrap, Mazaeus, allowed Alexander the Great to enter Egypt virtually unopposed, winning himself high office in Babylon for his pains.

Having assumed the mantle of his father, Phillip II of Macedon, the 20-year-old Alexander marched on the crumbling Persian Empire and defeated Darius III at the Battle of Issus in 333 B.C. A year later Alexander and his army entered Egypt. He visited the Oracle of Amun (Ammon) in the Siwa Oasis, famous in the Greek world, which duly proclaimed him the son of Amun-Re. He founded the city of Alexandria, the first and greatest of all the cities that were to bear his name, and did much to restore

A processional way leads to the famed Temple of Isis at Philae, now Agilkia Island at Aswan. Victorian travelers waxed lyrical over the beautiful island and its picturesque ruins. The Ptolemies built this most exquisite of temples with its finely decorated columns. Isis was a goddess so beloved of the Romans that the temple remained in use until A.D. 550.

the temples sacked by the Persians in their invasion 11 years earlier. Alexander may even have been crowned king at Memphis. The shrine at the Temple of Amun at Luxor was rebuilt on his orders and adorned with reliefs of Alexander making offerings to Amun-Min. But the restless Alexander never stayed long enough to fully occupy the throne of Horus. He resumed his Asian campaigning and died in Babylon in 323 B.C.

Conservative elements in Egypt resented the Greeks, other foreigners, and alien rule. As a result native Egyptians turned inward. Hieroglyphs became more cryptic and increasingly obscure, and the intricacies of Egyptian theology grew more convoluted, as the priests used the ancient beliefs as a bastion against foreign influence. Pilgrimages became popular, and above all, the common people became devoted to animal cults. The animals themselves were not worshiped but were revered for their association with particular deities. Baboons and ibises were associated with the god Thoth, cats with the cat goddess Bastet, and dogs with Anubis.

We should not be surprised by such reverence, for these were times of political confusion and decline when average Egyptians felt threatened by their loss of independence, their once proud position in the world. But they still had their own culture and private deities, which kept them identified as truly Egyptian. Their humble pilgrimages of personal devotion linked them to a familiar cosmos in a much more direct way than the vast and anonymous shrines of the great gods at Thebes and Memphis.

THE PTOLEMIES

Upon Alexander's death his generals divided up his empire among themselves. Ptolemy, son of Lagus, claimed Egypt, at first as satrap. On November 7, 305 B.C., he declared himself pharaoh. And Ptolemy's descendants ruled Egypt for nearly 300 years until the death of the famed Queen Cleopatra (Cleopatra VII) on August 12, 30 B.C.

The Ptolemies turned the Egyptian monarchy into very much a family affair. Each pharaoh appointed a son as his successor long before his death. Marriage within the family was an established institution. They considered themselves benevolent rulers presiding over a harmonious kingdom, giving themselves royal titles such as *Euergetes,* "benefactor," and *Soter,* "savior." Their courts were famous for their extravagance. A procession organized by Ptolemy II Philadelphus at a festival in honor of his father during the mid-third century included a mechanical float carrying a statue almost

13 feet high. The figure would stand up, pour a libation of milk from a golden vessel, then sit down again. Another float featured a winepress 36 feet long with no fewer than 60 people dressed as satyrs trampling the grapes. Greek and Macedonian customs strongly influenced court behavior in ways that would have shocked the conservative royal courtiers of the New Kingdom to whom customary protocol was all-important.

The Ptolemies considered themselves thoroughly modern rulers. They called themselves "Benevolent Gods," but there is no sign that they really thought of themselves as divine rulers like their ancient predecessors. Although the Ptolemies proclaimed themselves family men, constant intrigues swirled around the court. Sometimes the intrigues erupted in civil wars, pitting brother against sister, father against son. Ptolemy VIII Euergetes II so offended his subjects that he was forced to flee to Cyprus in 163 B.C. There he plotted his return to Egypt where his sister-wife Cleopatra II now ruled, murdering his son Memphites, dismembering him, and sending her the corpse. In 129 he invaded Egypt and seized the throne.

The later Ptolemies were almost as outrageous. Ptolemy X Alexander I, who reigned at the beginning of the first century B.C., ate and drank to such excess that he could not walk on his own without support. Ptolemy XI Alexander II married his aunt who had

inherited the throne but murdered her within a month of the wedding. He was lynched after a 19-day reign in 80 B.C.

For all its intrigues and violence Ptolemaic Egypt was an economic powerhouse. The Ptolemies controlled an enormous empire gained by diplomacy and military action, maintained by a powerful army and navy, and fought constantly with the Seleucid monarchs of Persia, themselves descendants of one of Alexander's generals, for control of strategic cities in Syria and the Levant.

ALEXANDRIA NEXT TO EGYPT

The prosperous and bustling delta was the economic hub of the kingdom. Strict citizenship rules ensured the Greek character of its cities. Delta townspeople spoke Greek and dressed in Greek clothes. Ships from all parts of the Mediterranean world docked in its ports. Heraklion was an important port in Alexander the Great's time and was still a much visited place of pilgrimage until its destruction by an earthquake in the eighth century A.D. A team of archaeologists under French underwater explorer Franck Goddio has located the site of the port 30 feet below the surface

This sandstone-encased mud-brick temple with more than 45 chambers—the only known Egyptian shrine dedicated to Alexander the Great, who conquered Egypt almost without resistance in 332 B.C.—overlooks Bahariya's Valley of the Golden Mummies. Zahi Hawass believes the farmers and merchants of Bahariya created their cemetery nearby so they could lie close to the legendary divine king forever.

about 4 miles offshore of modern Alexandria and has recovered coins and statuary.

Alexandria, the jewel in the Ptolemies' crown, soon surpassed Athens as the cultural center of the Greek world. Its founding citizens came from all over the Greek domain. Close to half a million people lived in the city during the first century B.C. Many people called it *Alexandria ad Aegyptum,* "Alexandria next to Egypt," for it was almost a country unto its own. The city stood 20 miles west of the Nile's westernmost mouth with a causeway linking Alexandria to the island of Pharos. On a rocky outcrop of the island was one of the Seven Wonders of the Ancient World, a lighthouse built in 280 B.C., said to have been 460 feet high with a square tower, a metal fire basket, and a statue of Zeus the Savior. Alexandria's library, the largest in the world, held hundreds of thousands of volumes and supported a community of scholars and poets from all over the Hellenistic world, among them the mathematician Euclid (ca 300 B.C.).

In 1992 Franck Goddio started charting the seabed of Alexandria's harbor, using as his starting point the Greek geographer Strabo, who had spent five years mapping the city shortly after Cleopatra's death. Earthquakes and tidal waves engulfed Strabo's Alexandria many centuries ago. Indeed magnetometers and other sonic devices now reveal a topography much altered by earth tremors. More than 3,500 exploratory dives have resulted in many finds—each one located precisely with the aid of a satellite-driven global positioning system (GPS)—cataloged, sometimes duplicated with underwater molds, and left in place. The remains of a ship 99 feet long, dating to the first century B.C. or slightly later, still lies in the royal harbor.

VALLEY OF THE GOLDEN MUMMIES

An antiquities guard's donkey stumbled into a hole in the Bahariya Oasis southeast of Cairo in 1996 and revealed the face of a mummy peering out of the sand. This find is one of the most spectacular archaeological discoveries ever made in Egypt. Bahariya was a wealthy farming and winemaking community 2,000 years ago. Her prosperous merchant families were buried in a long forgotten cemetery that covered nearly 14 square miles and was in use from about 332 B.C., the time of Alexander the Great, throughout Roman times, and into the fourth century A.D.

Egyptian archaeologist and Director of the Pyramids Zahi Hawass and a research team are investigating the Bahariya cemetery. By 1999 they had uncovered 105 mummies buried in family tombs, together with funerary ornaments, necklaces, ceramics,

A VALLEY OF GOLDEN MUMMIES

A wealthy man of about 50 and his wife, along with
41 other Bahariyans, rested in a multichambered tomb
(right) in the Valley of the Mummies. Coins to pay
the ferryman of the solar boat lie alongside a painted
mummy mask (above, top). A wooden panel behind
the mask shows Osiris crowned by Horus and Isis.
Statuettes of women (above) mourn the deceased.

Roman Egyptians of the first to third centuries A.D. commissioned portraits

for their mummies, now called the Faiyum mummies, like this one of a child

found in a cemetery at Hawara, north of Pharaoh Amenhotep III's pyramid.

FOLLOWING PAGES: Now crumbling, a Roman fort some 25 miles from

Bahariya Oasis once protected a major trade route of Egypt's Roman conquerors.

and even Greek and Roman coins. One sepulchre, Tomb 54, contained 43 mummies from several generations, lined up closely alongside one another. The most lavishly decorated, a man of about 50, was completely wrapped in linen with a cartonnage (layers of glued linen) chest plate, his chest and head covered in a layer of gold. A woman with identical adornment lay next to him, her head turned toward him as if gazing lovingly at her husband.

A gold-masked young man was wrapped in several layers of linen, then his head, shoulders, and upper body encased in cartonnage painted with traditional images of funerary deities. There are mummies of children, too, including a brother and sister, even a young woman who died shortly before her marriage, buried wearing a stucco mask painted to resemble the countenance of a bride, for the Egyptians believed she would be married in the afterlife.

EGYPT ADDED TO THE EMPIRE OF ROME

The Ptolemies were well aware of the growing power of Rome. In 170 and 168 B.C., Seleucid King Antiochus IV invaded the delta and eventually had himself crowned pharaoh at Memphis in the traditional manner. But in the summer of 168 a Roman ambassador arrived at Antiochus's headquarters near Pelusium and highhandedly ordered him to withdraw from Egypt. Antiochus asked for time to consult his advisers. In a menacing demonstration of Roman power the ambassador drew a circle around the king and told him to make a decision before he stepped out of it. The Seleucids duly withdrew in the face of diplomatic and military reality, for Rome was rapidly becoming the dominant force in the eastern Mediterranean world.

Egypt had maintained friendly diplomatic relations with the Romans for generations and had supplied grain to them. But after 168 B.C. Egypt's independence was at Rome's discretion and under her protection. The Ptolemies were now little more than Roman puppets and their country prospered as a client state. Roman politicians drooled over Egypt's wealth. In 65 B.C. Crassus and Julius Caesar contemplated making the country a province of Rome. Events played into their hands. King Ptolemy XII imposed such heavy taxes and fawned so heavily on Rome that his subjects expelled him. He fled to Italy and bribed Julius Caesar to obtain senate recognition of his right to the throne. Gabinius, the proconsul of Syria, gave him three legions to march on Alexandria. He regained the throne, murdered Queen Berenice IV, who had

Queen Cleopatra bore Julius Caesar a son, Caesarion. In this relief portrait she presents him to the gods at the Temple of Hathor at Dendera, in Upper Egypt. Caesarion became her co-regent Ptolemy XV before the Roman takeover in 30 B.C.

succeeded him, and ruled for four years, backed by a Roman military presence.

Ptolemy XII's daughter Cleopatra VII inherited the throne at age 17, on the understanding she would marry the elder of her two brothers, Ptolemy XIII. She learned of a plot on her life, fled to Syria, and returned at the head of an army, only to achieve stalemate outside Pelusium. Egypt now became embroiled in Roman power politics. Julius Caesar followed his hated rival Gnaeus Pompeius Magnus (Pompey) to Pelusium when he sought refuge with Ptolemy XIII. Pompey was promptly assassinated, and Ptolemy XIII drowned in a fight against the Romans on the island of Pharos. Cleopatra now married her younger brother Ptolemy XIV, while becoming Caesar's mistress and bearing him a son, Ptolemy XV Caesarion.

The Egyptian-speaking Cleopatra commanded respect, even if her country was a client of Rome. A clever and intensely political woman of great ruthlessness, Cleopatra realized her country was now a pawn in a much larger power struggle that erupted in the Roman Empire after Caesar's murder in the senate in 44 B.C. Inevitably Cleopatra became entangled in the intense rivalry between Gaius Octavius (Octavian) and Marcus Antonius (Mark Antony), who had divided the Roman Empire after the assassination of Caesar. Antonius summoned Cleopatra to a meeting in Cilicia, where she arrived in a state barge with purple sails and silver oars as soft music played, drenched in exotic perfume and dressed as Cupid. Mark Antony was dazzled. The pair immediately came together and lived in great style in Alexandria where their rowdy banquets kept the inhabitants awake all night.

Back in Rome Octavian waged an unrelenting propaganda war against Antony and obtained copies of confidential documents in which the couple divided Egypt and the eastern empire between their children. Rome authorized war, and a climactic naval engagement at Actium on September 2, 31 B.C., ended in defeat for Antony when Cleopatra's ships suddenly withdrew without warning. A year later Octavian entered Alexandria. Marcus Antonius fell on his sword, and Cleopatra committed suicide. Octavian ordered them buried in the royal tomb that Cleopatra had prepared for herself.

In a stela erected at Alexandria to commemorate the victory at Actium, an anonymous local poet proclaimed: "Caesar calmed the storm of war and the clash of shields ...and came rejoicing to the land of the Nile, heavy laden with the cargo of law and order and prosperity's abundant riches, like Zeus, the god of freedom." Octavian contented himself with one sentence: "I added Egypt to the empire of the Roman people." The land of the pharaohs had become a province of the Roman Empire.

Additional Reading

ALDRED, CYRIL. *The Egyptians.* Thames & Hudson, 1984.

BAINES, JOHN AND JAROMIR MALEK. *Cultural Atlas of Ancient Egypt.* Facts on File, 2000.

BUTZER, KARL W. *Early Hydraulic Civilization in Egypt: A Study in Cultural Ecology.* University of Chicago Press, 1976.

CLAYTON, PETER. *Chronicle of the Pharaohs.* Thames & Hudson, 1994.

DAVID, ROSALIE. *Handbook to Life in Ancient Egypt.* Facts on File, 1998.

DAVIES, VIVIAN AND RENEÉ FRIEDMAN. *Egypt Uncovered.* Stewart, Tabori & Chang, 1998.

FREEMAN, CHARLES. *The Legacy of Ancient Egypt.* Facts on File, Inc., 1997.

HAWASS, ZAHI. *Valley of the Golden Mummies.* Harry N. Abrams, 2000.

KEMP, BARRY J. *Ancient Egypt: Anatomy of a Civilization.* Routledge, 1989.

LEHNER, MARK. *The Complete Pyramids.* Thames & Hudson, 1997.

LICHTHEIM, MIRIAM. *Ancient Egyptian Literature: A Book of Readings,* Volumes 1&2. University of California Press, 1976.

MALEK, JAROMIR, ED. *Cradles of Civilization: Egypt.* University of Oklahoma Press, 1993.

REEVES, NICHOLAS. *Ancient Egypt: The Great Discoveries.* Thames & Hudson, 2000.

_____. *The Complete Tutankhamun.* Thames & Hudson, 1990.

REEVES, NICHOLAS AND RICHARD WILKINSON. *The Complete Valley of the Kings.* Thames and Hudson, 1996.

SHAW, IAN, ED. *The Oxford History of Ancient Egypt.* Oxford University Press, 2000.

SILVERMAN, DAVID P., ED. *Ancient Egypt.* Oxford University Press, 1997.

WATERFIELD, ROBIN. *Herodotus: The Histories.* Oxford University Press, 1998

WILKINSON, RICHARD. *The Complete Temples of Ancient Egypt.* Thames and Hudson, 2000.

Acknowledgments

National Geographic Books acknowledges the assistance of Director of the Pyramids Zahi Hawass, Cairo, Egypt; Stuart Tyson Smith, Ph.D., Assistant Professor, Department of Anthropology,University of California, Santa Barbara; consulting editors Michele Tussing Callaghan and Rebecca Lescaze; and the NGS Photographic and Imaging Laboratory, NG Maps, and the NGS Indexing Division.

Museum Acknowledgments

The National Geographic Society thanks the following museums for granting permission to Kenneth Garrett to photograph objects from their collections:

The Egyptian Museum, Cairo: p. 1, 14-15, p. 25, 31, 39, 40, 58 upper left, 67 lower right, 70, 81, 83-all, 102, 115, 122-123, 126, 127, 128, 132, 133, 136-137, 138-139, 142, 146-147, 149 153, 160-161, 10.63, 167, 172, 178, 192, 212, 214, 216-217, 219, 225, 237 top, 240, 247, 248,261, 278.

The Nubian Museum, Aswan: p. 27, 264

The Luxor Museum: p. 194 upper right, 201, 205

Egyptian Museum, Berlin: p. 206, 210-211

The British Museum, London: p.213 top

Metropolitan Museum of Art, New York: 213 center

Ashmolean Museum, Oxford: 213 bottom

Brian Fagan

Brian Fagan was born in England and studied archaeology and anthropology at Cambridge University. Since 1967 he has been a professor of anthropology at the University of California, Santa Barbara. Fagan is internationally known for his writings on archaeology and is the author of numerous books on such varied topics as the first settlement of the Americas, the Aztec civilization, and ancient El Niños. His books include a best-selling history of Egyptology, *The Rape of the Nile; Time Detectives;* and *Floods, Famines and Emperors.* He has previously written two National Geographic books, *The Adventure of Archaeology* and *Into the Unknown.* Fagan lives in Santa Barbara, California, with his wife and daughter and enjoys bicycling, kayaking, cruising, and cats.

Kenneth Garrett

Educated at the University of Virginia and the University of Missouri, photographer Kenneth Garrett specializes in archaeology, paleontology, and ancient cultures. He has photographed archaeological subjects worldwide for NATIONAL GEOGRAPHIC and has also published his work in many other magazines and books, including *Smithsonian, Archaeology, Fortune, Forbes, Time, Life, Audubon,* and *Natural History.*

Garrett wishes to thank the many scientists, inspectors, and curators who made the photographs featured in this book possible over the years. Dr. Ali Gaballah, chairman of the Supreme Council for Antiquities, has been most supportive in granting permissions for National Geographic to document the ongoing research in today's Egypt. The Directors of the Cairo Museum, Mohammed Saleh and Soheir el Sawy, provided access to their excellent curatorial staff for my work in their collections. Dr. Zahi Hawass and Dr. Salima Ikram gave generously of their time to supply the intellectual input for what needed to be included in this project photographically. Special recognition must go to NATIONAL GEOGRAPHIC Editor in Chief, William L. Allen, for his interest in pursuing the projects in Egypt that have formed the backbone of this book. Director of Photography Kent Kobersteen and Associate Director Susan Smith have supported me in my many journeys. And finally, I want to thank the illustrations editors with whom I have worked closely to shape the coverage, John Echave, Todd James, Elie Rogers, and John Agnone.

Library of Congress Cataloging-in-Publication Data

Fagan, Brian M.

Egypt of the Pharaohs / by Brian Fagan; photographs by Kenneth Garrett.

p. cm.

ISBN 0-7922-7294-3 (regular)—

ISBN 0-7922-7295-1 (deluxe)

1. Egypt—History—To 332 A.D.

2. Egypt—Antiquities. 3. Egypt—Pictorial works. I.
   Title: Egypt. II Garrett, Kenneth. III. Title.

DT83 .F16 2000

932—dc21   2001030107

Brian Fagan
Photographs by Kenneth Garrett

Published by the National Geographic Society

John M. Fahey, Jr., *President and Chief Executive Officer*

Gilbert M. Grosvenor, *Chairman of the Board*

Nina D. Hoffman, *Executive Vice President*

Prepared by the Book Division

Kevin Mulroy, *Vice President and Editor-in-Chief*

Charles Kogod, *Illustrations Director*

Barbara A. Payne, *Editorial Director*

Marianne R. Koszorus, *Design Director*

Staff for this Book

Martha Crawford Christian, *Project Editor and Text Editor*

John Agnone, *Illustrations Editor*

Marty Ittner, *Art Director*

Diana L. Vanek, *Researcher*

Jeanne E. Peters, *Contributing Editor*

Carl Mehler, *Director of Maps*

Joseph F. Ochlak, Gregory Ugiansky, and National Geographic Maps, *Map Research and Production*

R. Gary Colbert, *Production Director*

Richard S. Wain, *Production Project Manager*

Sharon Kocsis Berry, *Illustrations Assistant*

Mark A. Wentling, *Indexer*

Manufacturing and Quality Control

George V. White, *Director*

John T. Dunn, *Associate Director*

Vincent P. Ryan, *Manager*

Phillip L. Schlosser, *Financial Analyst*

Composition for this book by the National Geographic Society Book Division. Printed and bound by R. R. Donnelley & Sons, Willard, Ohio. Color separations by Quad Graphics, Martinsburg, West Virginia. Dust jacket printed by Miken Companies Inc., Cheektowaga, New York.

The world's largest nonprofit scientific and educational organization, the National Geographic Society was founded in 1888 "for the increase and diffusion of geographic knowledge." Since then it has supported scientific exploration and spread information to its more than nine million members worldwide.

The National Geographic Society educates and inspires millions every day through magazines, books, television programs, videos, maps and atlases, research grants, the National Geography Bee, teacher workshops, and innovative classroom materials.

The Society is supported through membership dues and income from the sale of its educational products. Members receive NATIONAL GEOGRAPHIC magazine— the Society's official journal—discounts on Society products, and other benefits.

For more information about the National Geographic Society and its educational programs and publications, please call 1-800-NGS-LINE (647-5463), or write to the following address:

National Geographic Society
1145 17th Street N.W.
Washington, D.C. 20036-4688 U.S.A.

Visit the Society's Web site at
www.nationalgeographic.com.

Library of Congress Cataloging-in-Publication Data appears on page 287.